The Lá GUIDEBOOK

MJ *Cullinane*

*Who looks outside, dreams;
who looks inside, awakes.*

~Carl Jung

*You can't wake up if you
don't go to sleep.*
~Wes Anderson

The Raven's Dream Tarot
Copyright © 2023 by MJ Cullinane

All rights reserved. No part of this book may be reproduced or transmitted in any form or by any means without written permission from the author.

PREPARING TO USE YOUR DECK

I don't know about you, but when I get a new deck, I am so excited that I just want to jump in and start using it right away. Like a child on Christmas morning, I rip open the box and sift through the cards one by one with delight looking for little hidden images or small details. I look at each image up close and then from a distance to get a feel for its unique energy. Each card holds power and tells a story, and it is in this initial meeting that I connect with all the personalities and their quirks that reside within the deck. Some of the cards create a warm, comforting feeling like that of a good friend, others come off strong and create friction.

I use various methods to clear negative energy that builds up over time on my decks, and that includes first clearing myself of any negative vibes. If I am not in a good space energetically speaking while cleaning my deck, it's like mopping the floor while wearing a big old pair of muddy boots! The shower (aka my portal to the beyond) is a great place to let bad vibes go down the drain. I imagine the water as pure light energy washing away all the murky mucky-muck that tends to build up over time. Another technique and not to go too far down the woo-woo hole here is to imagine that holding all that negative junk in your body is one of those rubber tub stoppers with a metal chain. Imagine it is near your belly button or Solar Plexus.

Now envision giving the metal chain a good tug until the rubber stopper comes out, and with it, you release all the emotional toxins that seep into our bodies as a result of just—well—living.

The sun, when present (I am in Seattle, so it's often hit or miss nine-months out of the year), is also an excellent resource for clearing away any negative energy. The power of its light is transformative, and it doesn't take long, nor does it require you to get naked (unless you are into that, and that is awesome too—you and Ben Franklin, in that case, have something in common.)

I find just ten to fifteen minutes sitting comfortably in the sun does a wonderful job of shifting my mood.

Cleaning the house and saging are two activities that, for me, go hand and hand. Not only do these activities make our home pleasant to be in, but it also raises the overall vibration. Saging I have found has a calming quality for both my child and pup Layla, so overall, it's a big win!

To clear a new deck or to clean a deck that has some negative energy build-up, I start by washing the cards. First, you spread the cards all over a table (image side down) and swish them around. Make sure they are nicely mixed up. Then let your intuition guide you around the table, picking up a card from one area then a couple from another.

When you have about a third of the cards in your hand, shuffle them until you feel ready to stop and then put that stack aside.

Go back to the table and pick up some more cards from various places until you have only a third remaining. Shuffle the cards and set them next to the first stack. Finally, gather the remaining cards and shuffle those as well. Stack the piles however you like and then shuffle the deck as a whole. If it is a full moon, that evening set the deck near a window that allows the moonlight to come in.

You may also want to keep your deck protected by using crystals such as clear quartz in your deck bag on the box.

Before you touch the deck of cards to do a reading, clear your mind. The goal is to transition into a space of feeling at peace and connected to divine energy. I find floral scents such as jasmine and rose help me escape from day to day stress and create a feeling of inner calm. You may find going for a walk is your path to your higher-self. Sometimes turning up the music and dancing can do wonders for disconnecting from stress. However, it is that you get to a place of peace; it is in the end up to you.

SINGLE CARD: YES / NO / MAYBE

To use the Förhäxa Tarot as an oracle simply think of a question that can be answered as a yes or a no. Shuffle the deck while you focus on your query. When you feel that little tug that lets you know the answer is ready to be revealed, draw your card.

Yes

The Fool
The Magician
The Empress
The Chariot
Strength
The Star
The Sun
The World

Ace of Fire	Ace of Water	Ace of Earth
Three of Fire	Two of Water	Three of Earth
Four of Fire	Three of Water	Nine of Earth
Six of Fire	Nine of Water	Ten of Earth
Eight of Fire	Ten of Water	Page of Earth
Page of Fire	Queen of Water	Knight of Earth
Knight of Fire	Ace of Air	Queen of Earth
Queen of Fire	Six of Air	Elder of Earth
Elder of Fire	Page of Air	
	Queen of Air	

No

The Council of Monarch
The Hierophant
The Hanged Man
Death
The Devil
The Tower
Seven of Fire
Ten of Fire
Five of Water
Two of Air
Three of Air
Five of Air
Seven of Air
Eight of Air
Nine of Air
Ten of Air
Elder of Air
Four of Earth
Five of Earth
Six of Earth

Maybe

The High Priestess
The Lovers
The Hermit
The Wheel of Fortune
Justice
Temperance
The Moon
Judgment
Two of Fire
Five of Fire
Nine of Fire
Four of Water
Six of Water
Seven of Water
Eight of Water
Page of water
Knight of Water
Elder of Water
Four of Air
Knight of Air
Elder of Air
Two of Earth
Seven of Earth
Eight of Earth

SINGLE CARD: ADVICE

Single card draws can be especially useful for rooting out problem areas or knots that keep your energy from flowing smoothly.

Quiet your mind and hold the deck in your hands firmly. You may have a specific question in mind, or you may want to see what information your guides or higher-self wish to convey to you at the moment. Shuffle the deck until you feel that little tug in your gut—pull a card. Sometimes the message comes across loud and clear, like when you are late putting food in your cat's dish! Other times, the message may come to you in a subtle tone that only begins to make sense after time. Then there are those times when—the message is so undeniable, yet we choose to ignore it.

I noticed with my Crow Tarot deck that the same card would appear over and over, and I believe the cats will be very similar as they too are persistent creatures. When this occurs, it is a message that your guides are trying to get your attention, and clearly, you must be either ignoring them or too much in denial to understand the first two or three times. I suggest making a chart and take note of the cards you pull each day.

I created this spread for when I do a reading for the collective. It's a great quick yet informative spread.

Influencing Energy: The energy that impacts your mood, decisions and relationships with others

Situation: What is coming up? Consider how does the influencing energy interact or influence the situation.

External Influence: Who or what is entering the situation. How does this energy contribute?

Wisdom: The wisdom the cards bring back to you that will help you reach move in the most beneficial direction.

REVERSALS

If you watch my daily readings for the collective, you probably have noticed I don't read "reversals"; instead, I let my intuition guide me as to the message my guides are offering when presenting me with each card. I tune into the energy and read what I feel. This is why I focus heavily on infusing each card with energy when I make my decks. My goal with every deck is for you to feel the card's vibration and read from there. It is here that the partnership with your guides is formed. Just as there are words in English that mean one thing in the US and something totally different in the UK, my guides speak to me using the vocabulary I understand. For example, imagine if someone who doesn't know you sent a message that read you need new trainers. You will be off to buy new running shoes in the UK, whereas here in the US, you might be on the hunt for a new coach. Your guides know you and will speak to you so that you understand. If my guides know this is my language and are loving, supportive entities, why *wouldn't* they talk with me in a language I understood?

Initially, I was drawn to Tarot over oracle cards when embarking on this journey because of each card's powerful energy, an energy that I found I could connect with. With 78 cards, there were plenty of opportunities for my guides to convey the message I needed. My approach to the Tarot is less strict than many traditional readers, primarily because I began this journey as means of connecting with my guides during a very tumultuous time. Our loving spirit companions aren't there to trip us up or provide false information because we don't speak "their" language. Our guides are here to help us navigate difficult situations not make matters worse.

My approach to reversals is this: If you agree with your guides that reversals are part of your communication, they will communicate using them; if not, they will speak without them. Receiving the information begins with creating a connection to your intuition. Aside from what direction the card is facing, what does your gut tell you? What message are you receiving when your mind is quiet, and your relationship with the divine is strong? At least, that is my opinion. Tarot and oracle decks are tools to tap into the Universe's energy. Just as spirit communicates using all of the languages in the world, the deck you choose tailors the messages to the individual.

QUESTIONS FROM THE MAJOR ARCANA

The Fool
"Are you letting the fears or opinions of others prevent you from taking a leap of faith?"

The Magician
"What is your magic power, and are you using it?"

The High Priestess
"When you tune in to the world around you, what do you see, hear, and feel?"

The Empress
"Are you aware of your position in this world—that you are a creator?

The Emperor
"Who holds you accountable?"

The Hierophant
"Are your traditions and beliefs a source of strength and inspiration, or do they keep you from expanding your knowledge?"

The Lovers
"Can you give yourself to another without losing who you are?"

The Chariot
"Are you in control of the situation?"

Strength
"Can you face adversity with grace and maybe a bit of humor?"

The Hermit
"Where do you feel most at peace?"

The Wheel of Fortune
"Are you playing roulette with your future, or are you making conscious positive choices?"

Justice
"Are the decisions you make today based on logic and wisdom, or are you letting expectations cloud your judgment?"

The Hanged Man
"Do your plans rely on others to help you move forward, if so, can you see your situation from their perspective?"

Death
"Can you find the beauty you hold within, that part of you that has been with you since birth?"

Temperance
"Where is the line between chaos and harmony meet

for you, and can you maintain your balance?"

The Devil
"What tempts you into a situation that may be less than desirable?"

The Tower
"Can you hear the rumble before a situation changes your life for good?"

The Star
"Are you able to see the brightness you have within —that part of yourself that deserves love and belonging?"

The Moon
"Are you showing off your authenticity, or are you trying to portray your vision of your ideal self?"

The Sun
"Will you allow yourself time to bask in the sun to recharge your spirit?"

Judgment
"Are you being transparent?"

The World
"Are you ready to hold the world in your hands?"

0. THE FOOL

Eventually, the raven succumbed to slumber, its belly fluttering with an unusual sensation akin to a swarm of butterflies taking flight. As it drifted deeper into sleep, a dream emerged from the shadows. The raven found itself observing a lively fox in pursuit of a flock of swallows, oblivious that it had strayed onto the beak and into the gaze of a raven. But even if it had known, the fox would have remained unperturbed. Nearby, a dog was barking, but the fox disregarded the noise, continuing its joyous frolic, seemingly uncaring that nestled just beneath lay a brood of famished fledglings. In this unencumbered creature, the raven recognized an audacious spirit and felt its radiating energy permeate its dream. Upon awakening, the raven felt a notable shift. The peculiar sensation of internal butterflies had vanished, replaced by the invigorating energy of the fox. It was as if this fearless creature's spirit was beckoning the raven onward, inspiring it toward its next exciting escapade.

New Beginnings: The Fool indicates you are on the precipice of a new journey, stepping into the unknown. This card may appear when you are ready for a fresh start or a new phase of life.

Innocence & Spontaneity: The energy of the Fool carries with it a childlike wonder and curiosity and may suggest your situation may benefit from approaching life with a beginner's mind. This energy is about spontaneous actions and decision-making without overthinking!

Fearlessness & Faith: The Fool does not shrink away from the unknown. Trust in the universe, the future, and your intuition. A leap of faith may be required.

Free-Spirited & Adventurous: You are reminded to embrace your adventurous spirit! The Fool reminds you to follow your heart and discover your path, regardless of what others think.

Potential & Possibility: Remember all options are on the table when the Fool appears. The energy of the Fool is a potent reminder of the infinite potential that resides within you and the myriad possibilities that life offers.

1. THE MAGICIAN

Besieged by an unresolved issue, the raven finally surrendered to the encroaching night, seeking solace in sleep. In its nest, the bird restlessly stirred until suddenly it found itself in an unexpected dreamscape, trapped within the cavernous belly of a whale. As the first flicker of panic ignited, the raven mustered the courage to quell its rising fear and channel its focus toward finding a way out. In the vast expanse of the whale's mouth, it discovered a few useful items: a sturdy stick, a container filled with flammable liquid, and the necessary materials to create a spark. With an unwavering mindset, the raven worked, concentrating all its energy on the singular goal of freedom.

Manifestation: The Magician reminds you of your ability to manifest your desires and realize your dreams.

Skill & Resourcefulness: The Magician symbolizes the ability to use your mental and physical capabilities to achieve desired outcomes. Your situation will benefit from being resourceful and pragmatic, utilizing whatever tools are available to create what you need.

Willpower & Initiative: You have the power to make things happen through your will and initiative. The Magician is a card of proactive energy and isn't about waiting for something to come to you.

Power & Influence: You are in a position to significantly impact your life and potentially others' lives as well.

Connection: The Magician signifies your ability to connect the material world with the spiritual realm.

2. THE HIGH PRIESTESS

Following a day fraught with stress, the raven slipped into the realm of dreams. There, it found itself ensnared by the gaze of an entrancing and enigmatic creature that bore an uncanny familiarity as if their paths had intertwined in a past life. Deep within her eyes, the raven discerned the secrets of the cosmos, solutions to the quandaries that had beleaguered its waking hours. Inhaling deeply, the raven held her stare, allowing itself to resonate with the pulsating energy that coursed around them. This was no mere dream, it realized, but a gateway to an underlying connection, a bond that was intrinsically part of its very being.

Intuition: The High Priestess calls upon your inner knowledge and a deep sense of intuition. She encourages you to trust your instincts. Pay attention to your feelings and dreams.

Mystery & Secrets: The High Priestess directs your attention to hidden aspects of a situation yet to be revealed. She embodies the unknown and the enigmatic, urging you to explore the depths of your subconscious.

Subconscious & Inner Voice: The High Priestess also represents the knowledge and wisdom from introspection and self-reflection.Your situation may benefit from slowing down and taking a second look.

Spiritual Enlightenment: The High Priestess symbolizes a spiritual journey or awakening. Now is the time to explore the spiritual dimensions of life and the divine knowledge within.

Feminine Wisdom: The High Priestess embodies divine feminine wisdom and encourages you to tap into your feminine side.

3. THE EMPRESS

After a lovely day of feasting and basking in the sun's warmth amongst its companions, the raven mused at the human's ironic labeling of their flock as an "unkindness," a stark contrast to their harmonious community. As the bird surrendered to a gentle slumber, it found itself in the presence of a raven with an aura of regality. Her energy radiated a serene and soothing ambiance reminiscent of a nurturing mother's caress.

In the dream, she watched over her egg with a loving gaze. Unexpectedly, one beak pierced the shell, followed by another, and yet another. Initially, the raven recoiled, the scene before it seeming unnatural. But it soon dawned on the bird that this majestic Empress held power to transform the mundane into the extraordinary, to manifest boundless abundance from a simple, ordinary object. She personified the potential for magnificence hidden within every small beginning.

Nurturing & Motherhood: The Empress embodies the power of creation, be it in the form of life, ideas, relationships, or artistic expression. She asks that you focus your energy on being a nurturer, offering love, care, and emotional support to those around you.

Abundance & Fertility: The Empress's energy offers abundance and asks that you reflect upon the richness of life. You can manifest a wealth of experiences, ideas, or relationships.

Nature & Sensuality: The Empress deeply connects with the Earth and the natural world. Her energy encourages you to appreciate nature's beauty and unite with your earthly roots.

Creativity: The Empress brings a fertile period of creativity. She encourages you to express your creative energy in art, music, writing, or any other creative pursuit.

Empathy & Compassion: As a mother figure, the Empress embodies a strong capacity for empathy and compassion. She encourages you to express love and understanding towards yourself and others.

4. THE EMPEROR

In its dream, the raven found its form expanding to envelop the vast expanse of the sky. Its majestic presence demanded reverence and awe, with wings so potent they could stir the elements of land and sea. Yet within, the raven felt a profound sense of duty, an inclination not towards destruction but creation. As the raven roused from its dream, its wings folded back into their familiar form, no longer vast enough to cradle the sky. Yet, the strength and responsibility it had experienced remained, not as a dream but as an awakening. The raven was infused with a renewed sense of purpose and accountability. The dream was not merely a flight of fancy but a transformative journey. Now wide awake, the raven was ready to embrace its new-found potential and navigate the world with its enriched perspective.

Authority & Leadership: The Emperor brings power, leadership, and authority. When the Emperor appears, it indicates a capability to take charge, make decisions, and enforce rules. With his energy supporting you, you can lead others with confidence and conviction.

Structure & Order: The Emperor may appear when there is a need to focus on the rules, systems, and principles that govern and help maintain stability.

Control & Discipline: The Emperor encourages you to control your surroundings, life, and destiny. This energy is about imposing order and setting achievable goals.

Stability & Foundation: The Emperor represents solid foundations and stability. His energy is about creating a secure and stable environment for growth.

Fatherhood & Protection: As a father figure, the Emperor symbolizes protective and nurturing qualities, ensuring the safety and welfare of others. He can also represent influence or guidance from a paternal figure.

5. THE HIEROPHANT

In its dream, the raven found itself amidst a gathering of youthful, zealous wolves, all attentively learning from an elder who embodied wisdom accumulated over many seasons. This seasoned pack member was imparting what it truly meant to bear the identity of a wolf, to understand the essence of collective harmony, and the importance of adhering to their way of life. The young wolves were learning to appreciate the rabbit as prey and as an integral part of their ecosystem, recognizing each creature's significant role within their community.

Tradition & Conformity: The Hierophant represents established social structures, institutions, and belief systems. It suggests a reverence for tradition, established protocols, and the necessity of working within specific societal frameworks.

Spiritual Wisdom & Guidance: Your situation may benefit from seeking spiritual wisdom and guidance. This card may represent a mentor or spiritual advisor who provides insight and advice. It's about seeking knowledge beyond the material and exploring the spiritual dimensions of life.

Morality & Ethics: The Hierophant may appear as a moral or ethical quandary. It suggests a situation where the right path is guided by established ethical principles or societal norms.

Religion & Belief Systems: The Hierophant may also indicate a desire to connect to something greater than yourself, often within organized religion or spirituality.

Education & Knowledge Sharing: The Hierophant may point to education and knowledge sharing. It often suggests a situation where wisdom is passed down or a need to seek formal education or training.

6. THE LOVERS

The raven surrendered to the soft pull of sleep. As the borders of reality blurred, a dream took form. The protagonist of this nocturnal drama was a solitary crow, perched on the rim of a bird bath, a shimmering oasis in a bustling cityscape. The crow had peculiar habits, including a fondness for cleanliness that extended to its prey. With meticulous care, it doused its food in the bird bath. Just as the crow was about to indulge in its carefully cleansed catch, a second crow fluttered onto the scene. It was a stranger, its eyes reflecting curiosity rather than hostility. It observed the loner with intrigue, its gaze shifting from the crow to the food and back again. The solitary crow, at first, contemplated shooing away this intruder. This was its bounty, won through careful planning and swift execution. But as it looked at the newcomer, it couldn't ignore the pang in its heart. The solitary crow realized the fellow crow wasn't driven by the desire to steal but by loneliness and the longing for companionship.

Love & Union: The Lovers represents romantic partnerships, deep affection, and a connection between two people. It's often a positive sign if you seek love or want to deepen an existing relationship.

Harmony & Balance: The Lovers may also symbolize harmony and balance within a relationship. It suggests a deep mutual connection, understanding, and equal partnership.

Choices & Duality: The Lovers may also appear if a choice or decision needs to be made. This choice usually involves matters of the heart but can also represent any situation where you must weigh different options that align with your values.

Values Alignment & Compatibility: You may need to consider if your values are in alignment with another. It encourages you to reflect on your personal beliefs and values and see if they align with your partner's or your choices.

Commitment: The Lovers represent a deep commitment, indicating a new level of responsibility in a relationship, such as engagement or marriage.

7. THE CHARIOT

The raven dreamt of two gleaming strings that bound themselves to its legs. The other ends of the strings attached themselves to the horns of an enormous, charging bull, bursting forth with the power of an unstoppable storm. The raven experienced a paradoxical mix of fear and excitement. The bull's determined charge toward the goal mirrored the raven's journey, their paths intrinsically connected. While fear tugged at the strings of its heart, the raven recognized the potential to achieve success. As the dream unfurled, the raven started to understand the significance of this strange encounter. This was not a trial or punishment but rather a call to action. It was an invitation to harness the bull's raw, earthly power, to ground its lofty aspirations with the solid strength of determined motion.

Determination & Willpower: The Chariot symbolizes determination, drive, and ambition. It suggests a time when you have a clear goal or purpose and the willpower to achieve it.

Control & Discipline: The Chariot represents controlling and maintaining discipline to keep things moving in the right direction. Balancing different aspects of your life and maintaining control over competing emotions or circumstances is crucial to achieving your goals.

Victory & Success: The Chariot often indicates success and victory, the triumphant result of hard work, self-discipline, and perseverance. It implies overcoming obstacles and that a positive outcome is within reach.

Self-confidence & Assertiveness: The Chariot symbolizes a confident, assertive attitude. It suggests a time to be bold and brave, to assert yourself, and remain confident in your abilities.

Journey & Direction: The Chariot can also represent a journey or progression, either physical or metaphorical. It signifies moving forward with purpose and direction.

8. STRENGTH

As night fell, the raven nestled into its perch, a sense of weariness washing over it. It had been a challenging day, filled with harsh squawks and pecks from the more experienced members of its flock. A feeling of isolation hung over it, much like the shadows cast by the settling dusk. There, in the ethereal landscape of its mind, stood a magnificent lion. Fear clenched the raven's heart, but it swallowed its terror and advanced. The raven found itself at the lion's face, their foreheads meeting in a moment of surreal connection. An indescribable energy flowed from the lion into the raven, transferring power, strength, and wisdom that coursed through its small body like a surge of electric warmth. The dream encounter with the lion had fortified its spirit with courage and instilled in it a profound understanding of the natural world's intricacies and a sense of empathy for the individuals that had sought to belittle it. Now, the raven faced a new day with a lion's heart and a compassionate soul.

Inner Strength & Courage: The Strength card symbolizes inner strength and resilience, often suggesting you have the internal fortitude to face life's challenges. It's not about physical strength but about emotional and spiritual strength.

Patience & Compassion: The Strength card also signifies patience, compassion, and understanding. It encourages you to approach situations with love and compassion rather than using force or control.

Control & Discipline: This card represents the ability to

control not just the situation but also one's emotions and instincts. It encourages the understanding and controlling of desires and emotions to reach your goals.

Fortitude & Resilience: Strength signifies the power of resilience, indicating that you can endure life's challenges and learn and grow from them.

Inner Harmony: The card suggests finding balance and alignment within yourself. It can represent a healing process and the need to forgive, to be kind to yourself, and to find inner peace.

9. THE HERMIT

As twilight melted into darkness, the raven surrendered itself to sleep, aching for solace and release from the constraints of its reality. It yearned for enlightenment but felt held down by invisible ties to its current circumstances. The raven dreamt of being guided toward a faint light glimmering. The spectral glow was its only beacon in the otherwise impenetrable darkness, offering a silent promise of something significant. Following the irresistible pull of the mysterious light, the raven made its way to a hidden cave on the side of a mountain. As it approached the cave, its heart pounded with trepidation and anticipation. The light source became more evident as it neared, revealing an astonishing sight. Standing at the mouth of the cave was a mirror image of the raven itself. However, this vision radiated an aura of wisdom and serenity that seemed to transcend time. As the raven woke from its sleep, the dream's imprint lingered.

The image of its older, wiser self remained, instilling a new-found determination. The raven received the message it was on a journey of transformation. With this revelation, the raven was no longer just a raven; it was a bird destined to soar above its trials, learning, growing, and forging its path toward becoming its wiser self.

Introspection & Solitude: The Hermit represents a period of introspection and self-reflection, often symbolizing a time to withdraw from the external world to explore your inner realm. This card encourages you to reflect on your life journey and personal growth.

Guidance & Wisdom: The Hermit often signifies seeking or imparting wisdom. This card could suggest that you are seeking guidance from a wise mentor or that you are the one guiding others.

Spiritual Enlightenment: The Hermit is closely associated with spiritual enlightenment and soul-searching. This card invites you to explore the depths of your spirit and connect with your higher self.

Soul Searching & Self-discovery: This card encourages deep introspection, pushing you to seek answers within. It's about understanding your core self and aligning yourself with your true values.

Contemplation & Searching for Truth: The Hermit's energy is about pursuing truth, understanding, and clarity. It's about pondering life's big questions and seeking truth in all forms.

10. THE WHEEL OF FORTUNE

As sleep enveloped it, the raven began to dream. It stood at the edge of a surreal landscape where a giant white rabbit, as luminous as moonlight, was at the center of the activity. With the wheel in front of it, the rabbit's soft paws manipulated the circular mechanism. Each wheel rotation initiated the delicate ballet of life, where seeds gently fell onto the fertile ground. With a touch of the rabbit's paw, the seeds sprouted and matured through various stages, eventually transforming into bountiful fruits. The fruits then decayed, giving way to new seeds, symbolizing the cyclical dance of life and death.

Fate & Destiny: The Wheel of Fortune often suggests that an important fate or destiny moment is at hand. It indicates that the forces of the universe are at work, offering significant changes that aligns with your destiny.

Cycles & Change: The Wheel of Fortune represents the cyclical nature of life and suggests that what goes around comes around. It's about the inevitable life changes, which can be for better or worse. The message here is to adapt to changes as they come.

Good Luck & Fortune: This card often signifies a turn of luck and indicates that good fortune or a happy surprise is coming. It's a reminder that fortune can turn on a dime and make the most of the good times while they last.

Karma: The Wheel of Fortune can also represent karma and understanding that your actions have consequences. It serves as a reminder that good deeds will lead to good outcomes and vice versa.

Uncertainty & Unexpected Events: The Wheel of Fortune might suggest unexpected events or changes, often reminding us that life is full of unpredictability and one must learn to navigate these circumstances.

11. JUSTICE

The raven slipped into a dream where an unexpected pyramid of creatures came into view. The bird was enchanted and felt a connection with each one. From the stag, it understood the importance of standing tall and using strength to protect its aspirations. The owl taught the bird to seek wisdom and face challenges with an open and questioning mind. The raven urged it to venture into the unknown and embrace the transformative experiences ahead. The silent yet powerful bat reminded the raven that there is life, activity, and potential for renewal even in darkness. The raven woke from the dream with a new-found understanding of its path. Each creature in the dream had shown the raven the way, shared its energy, and left an impression on its heart. Now, the raven knew it was ready for whatever came it's way, holding the lessons from her dream close.

Fairness & Balance: The Justice card represents fairness, balanced thinking, and equitable outcomes. It encourages a balanced perspective and the fair treatment of others. It suggests that actions have consequences, and decisions should be considered and deliberated.

Truth & Honesty: The Justice card is also about truth and honesty. It suggests seeking the truth in all matters and acting with integrity. It's a reminder, to be honest with yourself and others.

Law & Order: The Justice card can signify legal matters or official decisions. It may represent a legal judgment, a court case, or a dispute being settled. It advises that you must do what is legally and morally correct.

Accountability & Consequence: Justice speaks to the law of cause and effect. It suggests that you'll need to account for your actions and that you will face the consequences of your decisions.

Clarity & Rational Decision Making: Justice often points to the need for clear, rational, and balanced decision-making. It's about weighing all aspects of a situation to make a fair and informed decision.

12. THE HANGED MAN

In its dream, the raven soared high above an endless expanse of sand. Beneath it, wild white horses charged fiercely across the dunes, their manes flowing like liquid silver. Their rhythmic hoofbeats echoed the symphony of freedom, resonating with the raven's spirit of boundless flight. Suddenly, the rhythm of the dream shifted. In the midst of its reverie, the raven felt a jarring pull. An unexpected snake had latched onto its leg, drawing it forcefully down. The bird found itself hanging upside down, caught in the grip of an unforeseen obstacle determined to halt its progress. At first, the raven battled against its unanticipated predicament.

It struggled with the snake, its wings flapping wildly, its caw echoing across the dream desert. Yet, the more it battled, the tighter the snake's grip became. Succumbing to the snake's hold, the raven relaxed its body and stilled its wings. It allowed itself to hang, to view the world from this new perspective. When the raven woke up, it was with a renewed sense of understanding. It had gleaned a fresh perspective from its dream, learning that life's delays and obstacles could offer valuable lessons.

Suspension & Waiting: The Hanged Man represents a pause or delay in life, suggesting that there's a need to stop, wait, and see things unfold independently. This card encourages patience and understanding that not all things can be controlled.

Letting Go & Surrender: The Hanged Man speaks to the need to surrender to experiences or situations beyond your control. It's about accepting things as they are and releasing the need to try to change or manipulate situations.

Sacrifice: The Hanged Man often represents a necessary sacrifice - letting go of something in the present for future gain. This card teaches that sometimes you must put everything on hold before moving forward.

New Perspectives: The Hanged Man invites you to see things differently. A period of reflection and a change in outlook may be needed to understand a situation or yourself better.

Inner Harmony & Peace: Despite the somewhat distressing image, the Hanged Man is often seen as a card of peace and relaxation. It encourages finding peace within oneself and understanding life from a more spiritual perspective.

13. DEATH

In its dream, the raven stood in the shadow of an extraordinary creature - a colossal southern ground hornbill unlike any it had ever seen. It towered over the raven, its ominous silhouette creating a stark contrast against the ethereal light of the dream realm. What made it particularly peculiar were the two heads that rose, majestic and commanding, from its massive body. The heads had an eerie sense of unity about them. They moved together, gazes alternating between the myriad lives buzzing around them. Yet, each head had a distinct role in this strange world. The first observant and discerning head held the power to pick a life. It would stretch its long, strong beak into the bustling swarm of beings, selecting one at random with paradoxically purposeful precision. The plucked life was tossed to the second head. Unlike its counterpart, this head was transformative, with a sense of alchemical magic. As the first head passed the chosen life to it, the second would open its beak wide, engulfing the creature. The second head would let out a deep, resonant call, and the transformed life would emerge from its beak. No longer the being it once was, it would soar into the dreamscape, reborn, shining with new vitality, displaying characteristics it had never exhibited before.

Endings & Beginnings: The Death card represents the end of a significant phase or aspect of life and the start of something new. It's about closing one door to open another, signifying a meaningful, transformative change.

Transformation & Renewal: Death symbolizes transformation on a profound level. While this process can be painful, it often leads to renewal and greater understanding. The energy here is that of a metaphorical rebirth.

Release & Purging: The Death card encourages the letting go or purging of outdated beliefs, habits, or relationships that no longer serve your higher purpose. It's about letting go of the old to make way for the new.

Change & Transition: The Death card signifies unavoidable change, transition, or metamorphosis. It may be a sign that you need to change or that change is coming and beyond your control.

Acceptance & Surrender: The Death card also speaks to accepting what is dying or passing away. It teaches the wisdom of surrender, of releasing resistance to what is beyond your control.

14. TEMPERANCE

In the deep, dark silence of the night, as the moon bathed the land in its soft, silver glow, the raven nestled in the safety of the great oak tree, surrendering itself to sleep. The veil between realities thinned as it closed its eyes, allowing it to drift into a dreamscape of stunning grandeur. The dream transported the raven to a paradise beyond the realms of its ordinary existence. A lush garden stretched out in every direction, a symphony of vibrant colors and intoxicating fragrances. Blossoming flowers carpeted the Earth. A bubbling brook meandered through this floral tapestry, its waters glistening in the moonlight.

As the raven explored this mesmerizing realm, a sense of profound peace enveloped its heart. It was during this serene moment that it felt a presence, both familiar and divine, enter the garden. A second raven, radiant and pure, emerged from the sky. This otherworldly visitor radiated a light so loving, so pure, it felt as though it could touch and heal the soul's deepest wounds. Awakening from the dream, the raven felt a profound change within. The garden had vanished, and the divine raven was nowhere to be seen. Yet the peace it felt in the dream lingered, a radiant glow within its heart.

Balance & Harmony: Temperance represents equilibrium and balance. It encourages you to find middle ground and harmony in your life, suggesting a balanced approach to problems or challenges.

Moderation & Patience: Temperance often advises moderation in everything, urging you to avoid extremes. It can also represent patience and understanding that good things come to those who wait and take their time.

Healing & Renewal: Temperance often suggests a time of healing or rejuvenation. It may signal that you need to recover from a difficult situation or imply a time of spiritual or emotional healing.

Integration & Synthesis: Temperance often represents blending or synthesizing elements of your life to create something new or to find new insights. It speaks to the wisdom of integrating experiences and learning from them to create a harmonious whole.

15. THE DEVIL

When the young raven stumbled upon an open cage filled with the sweetest, most delectable peanuts, it could easily slip through the bars in case of any danger. In fact, it would come and go as it pleased regularly, always returning for a little taste when the desire called. One day while in the cage, a peanut dropped in. This peanut was even tastier than the original ones. It waited a moment, and another peanut fell from the sky and into the cage! What good fortune, thought the raven. But this peanut, although edible, was not nearly as good as the last one. So it waited. Another peanut fell. Again, not as good as the first one that fell from the sky. It stayed in the cage and waited, and again another peanut fell, and again it was not as good. The raven ate it anyway and waited for the next one. Over time, the raven grew bigger and bigger with each peanut until only its head could slip through the bars. In time, each peanut that fell became increasingly bland until they had lost all flavor, yet the raven, still searching for that original taste, kept eating until its body filled the cage's space, unable to move. The Devil never once locked the cage, but still, the raven was his.

Materialism & Sensual Pleasure: The Devil can represent an excessive focus on material wealth and physical pleasures. It could indicate overindulgence or living in excess at the cost of your spiritual well-being.

Bondage & Self-imprisonment: The Devil may indicate bondage or addiction, such as substance addiction, unhealthy relationships, or negative thinking patterns.

Temptation & Deception: The Devil can symbolize temptation and deception, often hinting at a situation or behavior that seems tempting but could have negative consequences.

Power & Control: The Devil can also represent power, control, or domination, either under someone else's control or exercising unhealthy control over others.

16. THE TOWER

The raven drifted to sleep, where its dream quickly morphed into a hellscape, flames licking the edges of reality, painting the world with their fierce, orange glow. The tranquil forest the raven knew so well was being devoured by an insatiable inferno, leaving only charred remains in its wake. The raven's home, a haven nestled amidst lush green, was swallowed by destruction. As the raven took flight, it saw a scattering of its brethren, their dark silhouettes cutting through the smoke, each one seeking safety in a different direction. A feeling of despair crept over the raven as it took in the burning devastation. But then, something shifted. Even in the depths of this dream-induced catastrophe, a realization dawned upon the bird - it was a harbinger, not just of doom, but of wisdom too. It acknowledged that this terrifying dream could also be a warning, a premonition of a potential reality. It behooved the raven to prepare, to consider all possible courses of action, to ensure the safety of its community.

Upheaval: The Tower may indicate a sudden, unexpected change or upheaval. This could manifest as a random event that disrupts the stability of your current situation.

Chaos & Destruction: The Tower is also associated with chaos and destruction, symbolizing the dismantling of existing structures, beliefs, or ways of life. This is often a necessary precursor to change and growth, even if it's uncomfortable at the time.

Revelation & Awakening: The Tower card can symbolize a revelation or sudden realization that changes your understanding of something. This is often a jarring experience but can lead to greater clarity and personal insight in the long run.

Release & Liberation: The Tower's energy often involves a release or liberation from something that's been holding you back. This can be an oppressive situation, limiting beliefs, or a life that no longer aligns with who you truly are.

Purging & Cleansing: The Tower card can represent a process of purging or cleansing. While this process can be uncomfortable, it often leads to renewal and transformation.

17. THE STAR

After a grueling day of tirelessly scouring for food under the harsh sun, the raven settled onto its perch, its heart burdened with survival struggles. The once flourishing forest gave way to desolation, and the bountiful food supplies had shrunk to a mere trickle. As sleep took over, the raven stood in a hauntingly familiar field - a poignant symbol of the world's growing harshness, stripped of its verdant lushness and replaced with barren desolation. Suddenly, the tranquil silence was broken by the fluttering of wings, echoing in the stillness like a distant melody.

A radiant raven, glowing with a celestial aura, descended from the heavens. It selected a star and tore it open with its sharp claw, releasing a cascade of twinkling stardust that danced down onto the barren land. Each speck of stardust was a seed of life, and as they touched the arid soil, a magical transformation began to occur. Awakening from its dream, the raven felt the stress of the previous day lift. The dream, although ephemeral, had gifted the raven with a renewed sense of purpose and optimism. As it gazed out into the early morning, the memory of the divine raven and the magically transformed field inspired the raven to face the day's challenges with renewed vigor and to work harder to find ways to overcome the growing adversities.

Hope & Inspiration: The Star is a symbol of hope and inspiration. It encourages optimism and a positive outlook, promising better times ahead. It is a light in the darkness, illuminating your path and giving you guidance and direction.

Faith & Serenity: The Star suggests a time of peace, healing, and tranquility. It brings an energy of serenity and reminds you to trust the process of life.

Renewal & Healing: The Star card often suggests a period of renewal and healing. After the turmoil the Tower symbolizes, the Star is a welcome card indicating rejuvenation, recovery, and a return to a sense of peace and balance.

Generosity & Openness: This may be a time to share your gifts or blessings with others, or it could be a time to be open to receiving blessings from the universe.

Goals & Aspirations: The Star also represents goals and aspirations, providing guidance and inspiration as you work towards your dreams. It's a reminder to stay true to your inner voice and personal vision.

18. THE MOON

In the grip of an unsettling dream, the raven stood amidst the shallow, cloudy waters of a forgotten lake. Its beak was caught firmly in the grip of a defiant crawfish, stubbornly refusing to release its hold. The moon's pale light reflected on the water's surface, casting ghostly images that appeared like skeletal remains, a sight that filled the raven's heart with an eerie unease. In the sky, the moon, the only light source in the nocturnal expanse, began to fracture. As the moon shattered, a gathering of ravens emerged from within, their ominous silhouettes stark against the crumbling lunar light. Their eyes pierced the raven's soul, invoking its deepest, darkest impulses. Awakening from its dream, the raven felt a sense of profound understanding. The dream was a metaphorical journey, reminding it of the constant struggle between the light and darkness within oneself. It served as a reminder that while it's easy to be swayed by one's worst tendencies, true power lies in acknowledging these shadows and choosing the path of resilience, hope, and courage.

Intuition & Dreams: The Moon represents the realm of the subconscious, dreams, and intuition. It encourages you to pay attention to your dreams and subconscious insights, which may carry important messages.

Illusion & Deception: The Moon can also symbolize illusion and deception. Things may not be as they seem, and you may need to look deeper to perceive the truth. It encourages you to question the reality of the situation and not take everything at face value.

Fear & Anxiety: The Moon often brings out fears and anxieties, the "things that go bump in the night." It can symbolize a time of uncertainty, confusion, and fear, often related to your mental and emotional states.

Reflection & Change: The Moon is associated with the feminine and the ebb and flow of emotions and states of being. It can signal a time of reflection, change, and the need to adapt to shifting circumstances.

Unconscious & Shadow Self: The Moon can represent your unconscious or "shadow" self. This card invites you to delve into your subconscious and confront aspects of yourself that you may not be fully aware of.

19. THE SUN

The raven spotted a lake of fire that shimmered like a mirage, its dancing flames the sole source of illumination in the vast inky expanse. Summoning its courage, the raven dove towards the molten lake, its wings unfaltering in the face of the intense heat. As it swooped over the fiery surface, it opened its beak and scooped up the blazing lava, molding it into a glowing sphere of radiance. With a powerful beat of its wings, the raven ascended from the lake, the ball of fire held steadfastly in its beak. As the raven ascended, the veil of darkness began to part, revealing the majesty of the celestial bodies.

Seeing the moon's silvery elegance, the stars twinkling like a thousand diamonds strewn across the sky, brought joy and pride to the raven. The once-forgotten lake of fire had been the catalyst to life, light, and warmth, and the raven, the unlikely messenger of light, the celestial architect who had carved beauty into the canvas of the world. In the dawn of the new day, the raven stood as a symbol of creation, hope, and transformation, forever changing the course of life with its fiery resolve.

Joy & Optimism: The Sun represents happiness, joy, and optimism. It symbolizes a time of celebration, positive energy, and abundant opportunities.

Success & Accomplishment: The Sun often indicates success and accomplishment. It can signal a time when you're achieving your goals, enjoying success, and reaping the rewards of your efforts.

Enlightenment & Clarity: The Sun can represent a time of enlightenment and understanding, where things that were once confusing or hidden are now clear. It can indicate a moment of great insight or a time when things are being revealed.

Vitality & Energy: The Sun is a source of life, warmth, and energy. When this card appears in a reading, it may indicate a time of rejuvenation, health, and vitality. It's a sign of being energized and full of life.

Positivity & Assurance: The Sun radiates positivity and assurance. It's a sign that things are going in the right direction. It's about feeling confident, enthusiastic, and assured in your path.

20. JUDGMENT

The raven dreamt of two celestial hummingbirds bathed in divine light's soft glow, letting out a harmonious cry that echoed across the dreaming landscape. It was a sound not of this world, a melody imbued with an undeniable energy of transformation and renewal. As their enchanting song filled the air, the raven felt a profound stir within its body. The raven's old, dust-coated feathers began to tremble with each note that vibrated through the air. They rustled and ruffled, dancing to the rhythm of the hummingbird's song until they began to detach one by one. Once integral to its flight, the old feathers transformed into vibrant new plumes, a testament to its rebirth. Once tired and worn, the raven was reborn, rejuvenated by the hummingbirds' magical song. With a grateful heart, the raven took to the skies, its new feathers catching the luminescent glow of the divine hummingbirds' realm. A sense of freedom and lightness enveloped the raven, and it realized the power of release, of letting go of the old to make way for the new.

Evaluation & Reflection: Judgment represents a time of in-depth assessment and reflection. It indicates that you are at a point where you need to understand and evaluate your past actions and decisions in light of your present situation.
Rebirth & Renewal: The Judgment card is often associated with a sense of rebirth or renewal. It symbolizes a point of significant change or transition, which can feel like a resurrection or rebirth into a new phase of life.

Inner Calling & Realization: Judgment can also represent an inner calling or realization. It's a wake-up call, urging you to listen to your inner voice or higher self. This could be a call toward your true purpose or vocation.

Forgiveness & Absolution: The Judgment card can indicate a time of absolution or forgiveness towards yourself or someone else. It's a reminder that everyone can change and start anew.

Spiritual Awakening: Judgment can signify a spiritual awakening or realization. It's about coming to a new understanding of yourself and the world around you. This card suggests that you are rising up and moving closer to your higher self and purpose.

21. THE WORLD

In its dream, the raven embarked on an odyssey from its tender years as a fledgling, untouched and naive to the world's complexities. Journeying through the tapestry of life, it tasted both the sweetness of victory and the bitterness of defeat, savored the warmth of love, and bore the sting of betrayal. With time, the raven learned to make peace with its past, embracing acceptance and forgiveness. In this dream, the raven found itself delicately poised on the cusp of two worlds - the past and the future. It was that fleeting, pivotal moment where one chapter had to close for a new one to unfurl.

Completion & Accomplishment: The World represents the completion of a cycle or a significant accomplishment. It indicates that a major chapter in your life has ended, and you are ready to start a new one.

Integration & Wholeness: The World suggests a state of wholeness and integration. It's about successfully bringing together all the lessons learned from the previous cards of the Major Arcana and achieving a state of balance and understanding.

Fulfillment & Success: This card is about achieving your goals and aspirations and feeling fulfilled in all areas of your life. It's about enjoying the fruits of your labor and recognizing your successes.

Enlightenment & Cosmic Consciousness: On a more spiritual level, the World card represents reaching enlightenment or cosmic consciousness. It symbolizes the end of a spiritual journey, having grown, evolved, and learned life's critical spiritual lessons.

ACE OF WANDS

The raven dreamt it was in the heart of the arid desert. A claw materialized, cradling a blazing phoenix within its grasp. Each beat of the phoenix's fiery wings ignited explosive surges of energy that infiltrated the raven's subconscious, infusing it with an invigorating eagerness.

The rhythmic flaps gave birth to a vibrant cascade of innovative ideas, flowing into the raven's mind like a river breaking free from its dam. This potent rush of inspiration flooded the raven's dreamscape, saturating every crevice of its thoughts with a powerful blend of imagination and purpose. As the raven stirred from its visionary slumber, an electric energy pulsed. Awake and brimming with a rejuvenated spirit, the raven found itself primed and eager to bring the innovative notions from its dream into reality.

New Beginnings & Potential: The Ace of Wands typically signifies a new beginning. It could represent a new project, career path, creative endeavor, or fresh start. It's about potential and the promise of future success.

Inspiration & Creativity: The Ace of Wands is often associated with a surge of inspiration or a creative spark. It's a powerful card for creative pursuits and suggests a time of increased energy and passion for new ideas.

Enthusiasm & Energy: This card is associated with high energy, confidence, and excitement. It's about seizing the moment, feeling inspired, and having the drive to pursue your passions.

Growth & Personal Development: The Ace of Wands can also suggest personal growth and development. It might indicate when you're discovering new aspects of yourself or exploring new areas of personal interest.

Boldness & Initiative: The energy of the Ace of Wands is bold and encouraging. It advises you to take initiative, be assertive, and act confidently.

TWO OF WANDS

In the hushed silence of the evening, a solitary raven succumbed to the lull of sleep. In its dream, the raven watched as a jealous night, coveting the radiance of the day, snuffed out its brilliant flame, shrouding the world in unending darkness.

In its dream, the raven felt bold, powerful, and undeterred by the encroaching night; it bore the audacity of hope. The raven knew what it needed to do - carry the fiery flower, the essence of daylight, and set the sky ablaze with the sun's glow again.

Planning and Future Ambitions: This card often appears when considering your long-term goals and entering the planning stage. The energy of this card encourages strategic thinking and making detailed plans for what you want to achieve.

Progress: The Two of Wands indicates that you are progressing with your plans, and there is a sense of progress. The energy of this card is positive for advancement and personal growth.

Discovery: This card often shows up when you are about to embark on a journey of discovery, either physically or mentally. It suggests an energy of exploration and expanding your horizons.

Decision Making: The Two of Wands may also appear when you have a decision that involves a commitment of some kind. This decision can be tough, but the card's energy supports a confident choice.

Personal Power: This card indicates a time of self-confidence and personal power. It suggests you are taking control of your destiny, using your strengths and resources to create your desired future.

THREE OF WANDS

Immersed in the realm of dreams, the raven imagined itself nestled at the base of an immense cavern, enveloped by rocky walls seemingly piercing the cosmos. It observed as the other creatures — birds, both great and small — fluttered about within their limits. Their flight patterns were predictable, always venturing to the precipice but never daring to cross it.

Piqued by an insatiable curiosity to discover what lay beyond the intimidating ledge, the raven committed itself to strengthening its wings until it was ready to ascend beyond the cavern's highest peak. Above the pinnacle, a panorama unfolded. An expansive tapestry of lush, unexplored lands, shimmering seas, and undiscovered terrains stretched beneath the bird. A vista of endless opportunities unfolded before its eyes, promising countless adventures and new stories to weave.

Preparation: The Three of Wands may appear when being prepared will help a situation. It may show up when you're getting ready for something significant in your life. The energy of this card encourages preparing, organizing, and laying down the groundwork for your plans.

Foresight and Vision: This card represents the ability to look ahead and plan for the future with wisdom and foresight. It indicates that you're able to foresee upcoming opportunities and challenges, and this vision will guide your decisions and actions.

Expansion: The Three of Wands is about expanding your horizons, often beyond the familiar. This could be in a literal sense, such as traveling or exploring new places, or in a figurative sense, such as expanding your mind or understanding of yourself and the world.

Progress and Growth: This card signifies progress towards your goals and personal growth. It's a positive indication that you're progressing and growing as an individual.

Optimism and Confidence: The energy of the Three of Wands is inherently optimistic and confident. It suggests that you have a positive outlook on your future and trust your abilities to make your vision a reality.

FOUR OF WANDS

The raven was immersed in a dream of a balmy summer evening illuminated by the enchanting glow of fireflies. The raven could almost feel the warmth of harmony enveloping it as if the entire woodland was united in a grand, spontaneous celebration. The normally silent shadows were now alive with gentle whispers, the rustling leaves, and the lyrical chirping of nocturnal creatures, each adding their unique voice to this jubilant chorus. The dream evoked a sense of deep connection and unity, creating a magical atmosphere where every creature, the raven included, was part of a grand, communal dance beneath the stars, all participating in the radiant celebration of life.

Celebration: The Four of Wands is known as a card of celebration. It's often associated with joyful events like weddings, reunions, or parties.

When this card appears, it's a sign of a time of happiness and joy, a pause to enjoy the fruits of your labor.

Harmony: This card indicates a time of unity and peace. It's about balance, and the feeling of tranquility that comes from knowing things are as they should be. This might mean internal harmony or harmony in your relationships or surroundings.

Home: The Four of Wands is often associated with the concept of home. This can be a physical home, a comfortable and secure environment, or a metaphorical home - feeling at home within yourself or your relationships.

Completion: This card may also signify an achievement. It might mean you've completed a project, achieved a goal, or reached a significant milestone. This is a card of accomplishment and pride in what you've done.

FIVE OF WANDS

The raven dreamt of being at the beach, joined by four unfamiliar raven companions. It wasn't long before their attention collectively riveted to a singular, commanding presence — a giant crab scuttling defiantly across the sandy expanse. The sight of the crab sparked a fervor among the group, igniting their competitive spirits. No longer were they mere companions sharing the beach but adversaries locked in an intense contest. The crab, an enticing prize in their eyes, became the focal point of their rivalry, transforming their tranquil gathering into a dynamic battlefield. Feathers ruffled in the tension, wings spread in assertive displays, and squawks of challenge echoed across the beach. The dream became a stage set for an intricate dance of ambition and competition, each bird vying to claim the grand prize — the majestic delectable crab.

The dream became a stage set for an intricate dance of ambition and competition, each bird vying to claim the grand prize — the majestic delectable crab.

Conflict: The Five of Wands frequently represents a disagreement or clash of ideas or interests. It might be an internal conflict—where you're battling with yourself—or it could refer to an external conflict, perhaps a disagreement or rivalry with others.

Competition: This card might appear when you are facing competition, possibly in your professional life. This competition might be friendly or more intense, but it usually signals that you're being challenged or tested.

Tension: The energy of the Five of Wands often indicates a time of tension or stress. This could be due to a conflict or simply a challenging situation that is causing you to feel strained or pressured.

Chaos: The Five of Wands can symbolize chaos or confusion with many competing forces at play. This might be a time when things feel like they need to be more organized.

Growth through Challenge: Despite the challenging energy of the Five of Wands, it's also a card of growth and development. You can learn, adapt, and grow stronger by dealing with conflict and competition.

SIX OF WANDS

In the realm of dreams, the raven experienced what felt more akin to a prophetic vision. It stood amidst an ocean of sunflowers, their golden faces swaying gently in the breeze. The atmosphere infused the raven with an airy buoyancy and a powerful sense of confidence. The air buzzed with an almost palpable promise of impending triumph. Without warning, a swirl of pristine white moths erupted from the verdant carpet of sunflowers. They spiraled upwards, their delicate wings whirring rhythmically, choreographing a dance of life around the raven. In a moment that defied reality, these gentle creatures lifted the bird, their multitude creating a platform for the raven. They carried it above the sunflower canopy, presenting a panoramic view of what lay beyond. The sight unfurled before the raven was a testament to the promise of success that the field of sunflowers had hinted at. The dream was a surreal harbinger, suggesting that fortune and achievement were not merely on the horizon but within the raven's reach, ready to be embraced.

Victory and Success: The Six of Wands is primarily a card of victory. It's a sign of triumph over adversity, obstacles, or challenges. When this card appears, it's a positive sign that you're moving towards a successful outcome.

Recognition and Praise: This card often signifies glory or praise from others for your achievements. It could mean public recognition, like an award or promotion, or a personal acknowledgment from someone close to you. It carries the energy of validation for your hard work.

Self-Confidence: The Six of Wands is also about self-confidence and personal pride. This card represents feeling good about your achievements and being proud of your accomplishments.

Progress: The appearance of this card also indicates progress. It suggests that you're moving forward, leading you to success. It's a sign that things are going in the right direction.

Leadership: The Six of Wands can indicate that you are in a leadership position, or it might suggest that now is a good time to step into a leadership role. It speaks to the respect and admiration that others have for you, which positions you well to guide and influence others.

SEVEN OF WANDS

The raven dreamt of feeling hungry. Its gaze set upon a nearby crab, its potential feast. Just as the raven was about to snatch up its coveted prize, a tentacle, as unsettling as it was unexpected, emerged from the water. The raven, taken aback but undeterred, edged a little closer to the crab, its resolve unbroken. Yet, the sea had more surprises in store: another tentacle materialized from the waves, then another, and another still. The sight was alarming, escalating the raven's initial concern to a full-blown apprehension. Fear coursed through the raven's veins for a fleeting moment, its heart pounding a frantic rhythm against its chest. Yet, just as quickly as it had arrived, the fear dissolved, replaced by a wellspring of courage that surged through the raven's being. It took a deep breath, bolstering its bravery, and stood its ground. The raven would be enjoying crab that evening!

Defensiveness: The Seven of Wands often depicts a scene where one is standing their ground against opposing forces. This card may appear when you feel the need to defend your position, beliefs, or decisions, possibly from many angles.

Courage: To stand up to challenges and opposition, one must display courage. The Seven of Wands carries the energy of courage and bravery, showing the strength you possess to face adversity head-on.

Resilience: The card is a symbol of strength and persistence. It represents the determination and willpower to persist despite obstacles and opposition, and it shows that one can overcome adversity through resilience.

Advantage: Despite depicting a challenging situation, the Seven of Wands suggests you have the upper hand or an advantageous position. This card indicates that if you stand firm and hold your ground, you're likely to prevail.

Challenge: In a more general sense, this card signifies facing a challenge. It's a call to rise to the occasion, stand firm in your convictions, and meet whatever situation is at hand with strength and determination.

EIGHT OF WANDS

The raven was caught up in a dream of soaring through a star-speckled sky, each brilliant streak of a shooting star adding a sense of wonder and magic to its journey. During this serene flight, the unexpected happened: eight falcons, with their sharp eyes and mighty wings, dove from the heights, crossing paths with the raven. With their swift, synchronized movements, the falcons caught the raven up in their current, their rapid descent whisking the raven across the sky in a heady rush. Each falcon released a cryptic message into the wind. The words were hasty, lost amidst the rushing air. The raven found itself in a balancing act, struggling to decipher the messages while maneuvering skillfully to avoid a mid-air collision. The challenge was not merely physical, demanding agility and alertness, but also mental, requiring sharp focus and understanding. It was a dream that tested the raven's mettle, pushing it to hone its instincts and adapt to its nocturnal flight's thrilling, unexpected twists.

Rapid Movement and Progress: The Eight of Wands often represents swift action, rapid developments, and fast progress. It indicates a flurry of activity that propels you forward to achieve your goals.

Swift Change: This card is also associated with sudden change. This might be a new opportunity that comes out of nowhere, a sudden shift in circumstances, or a fast-paced transition.

Communication: The Eight of Wands may also represent communication. This might refer to rapid information exchanges, quick decisions, or messages coming your way. It could indicate that you'll soon receive news or important information.

Energy and Enthusiasm: The Eight of Wands carries an energy of excitement, enthusiasm, and high energy. It's a card that encourages you to go for it and fully invest in whatever you do.

NINE OF WANDS

Within the folds of a dream, the raven envisaged a state of contentment that was the sweet fruit of its ceaseless labor. The bird had toiled endlessly, crafting a haven brimming with abundance and happiness, and was on the cusp of embracing the joys of parenthood. Just when it was about to sink into the plush comforts of its hard-earned success, an unexpected sight caused it to jolt upright. Two falcons were hovering menacingly over its nest, their intimidating presence causing the raven's feathers to bristle in alarm. Despite the wave of exhaustion that washed over it, the raven was not about to relinquish the rewards of its diligent work. Fueled by its desire to protect its haven and the imminent arrival of its offspring, energy pulsed within its veins. Mustering every ounce of strength it had left, the raven steeled itself, preparing to ward off any threat and defend the sanctuary it had painstakingly built.

Resilience: The Nine of Wands often appears when you've been through a series of challenges and have shown great resilience. You've withstood the test of time, and while you may be weary, you're still standing. This card acknowledges your persistence and toughness.

Determination: This card carries the energy of determination. Despite the challenges and setbacks, you're determined to continue and reach your goal. This determination is a source of strength and will help you push through the final hurdles.

Guardedness: The Nine of Wands can also suggest a feeling of being on guard or the need to protect what you've worked hard to create. You've come this far and will not let anyone or anything take away your progress.

Final Push: The Nine of Wands often appears when you're in the final stages of your journey or project. It's been a long road, but the end is in sight. This card encourages you to muster your remaining energy for this last leg.

Inner Strength: The Nine of Wands may suggest a situation requiring inner strength. It may be difficult, but know that you have the fortitude to withstand these challenges and reach your goal!

TEN OF WANDS

Deep within a dream, the raven envisioned a lustrous net submerged in the water, seemingly brimming with fish. With visions of a grand feast lasting for days, it dove down, intending to haul the net to the shore.

Yet, the dream twisted. The multitude of fish began to morph and meld into one another. In the blink of an eye, the net no longer housed a school of fish but a colossal whale. Even though the situation defied reality, the raven, being in the throes of the dream, doggedly continued to yank at the net, wrestling to hoist the enormous creature from the watery depths.

Then, an octopus appeared as if the whale wasn't enough! Its tentacles reached out, wrapping around the whale and pulling it back toward the sea. The raven's task now escalated from merely impossible to utterly surreal. Yet, it stubbornly persisted, matching each tug of the octopus with an equally determined pull. Just as it seemed the raven was gaining an inch of progress, the spell of the dream broke, and it jolted awake. Rather than feeling rested, the raven woke up feeling even more fatigued than before its slumber, as if the dream's strenuous tugging battle had somehow seeped into reality.

Burden: The Ten of Wands is frequently associated with the feeling of being burdened. This could result from taking on too much responsibility, trying to do everything at once, or refusing to delegate tasks.

Hard Work and Responsibility: This card often appears when you're working hard and carrying a heavy load. While the effort you're putting in is commendable, the Ten of Wands also reminds you to manage your responsibilities effectively.

Struggle: Given your heavy load, the Ten of Wands can indicate a struggle. This could manifest as feeling overwhelmed, overworked, or exhausted from juggling too many tasks simultaneously.

Persistence: Despite the struggles and burdens, the Ten of Wands can also symbolize persistence. It's about pushing through, even when times are tough.

Completion: As a ten, this card also symbolizes the end of a cycle. It may suggest that you're nearing the completion of your task or project. The end is in sight, even if it's an uphill battle to get there.

PAGE OF WANDS

The raven dreamt of a fledgling brimming with boundless vitality and a daring spirit of exploration. The young bird embodied curiosity, eager to experience all the world had to offer. The fledgling spotted a tiger just about to devour a fish. The desire to participate gripped the young raven, its boldness overshadowing any trace of fear or reservation.

Rather than responding aggressively, the tiger found itself struck by the audacious enthusiasm and sheer innocence radiating from the youthful bird. Its eyes softened, and an understanding passed between the two unlikely companions. Gently, the tiger extended its massive paw, creating a perch for the raven. In a display of surprising camaraderie, the mighty beast shared its meal with the bird. It was a surreal scene: a testament to the young raven's fearless spirit and a strange yet beautiful alliance formed in the depths of a dream.

Exploration & Discovery: The Page of Wands often represents the beginning of a journey of exploration and discovery. It can indicate a period where you seek new experiences, explore new ideas, or push your boundaries.

Excitement & Enthusiasm: This card is associated with excitement, enthusiasm, and youthful energy. You may feel driven by your passions and desires, eager to pursue new opportunities, and full of optimism.

Confidence & Boldness: This card is also about confidence and boldness. It suggests a time when you're feeling confident, bold, and ready to take on the world.

Freedom & Adventure: The Page of Wands is about freedom and adventure. It signifies a free spirit, someone who values their independence, loves adventure and isn't afraid to step out of their comfort zone.

Creativity & Inspiration: In relation to creativity, the Page of Wands represents a time of initial inspiration. This card is about the spark that starts the fire, the first step in a creative journey, or the first note of a new composition.

KNIGHT OF WANDS

The raven roused from a bizarre dream that had left its little heart pounding. It had formed an unlikely camaraderie with a delicate white rabbit. However, the tranquillity of their friendship was threatened by the ominous presence of a mountain lion stealthily closing in on the unsuspecting rabbit. Without hesitation, driven by a sense of protection over its newfound friend, the raven descended from its safe perch upon a tree. It filled the air with loud, defiant caws, aiming to distract the predatory cat. The lion's attention drawn by the raven decided that a bird would make an equally satisfactory dinner. Despite the approaching danger, the raven stood resolute, its caws growing louder and more fervent. The lion needed merely to execute a single swift swipe of its lethal paw, and its razor-sharp claws would inevitably ensnare the daring raven. The raven's heart thrummed wildly in its chest as it awaited the lion's attack while keeping its eyes trained on the rabbit. As soon as it discerned that the rabbit had made it far enough to safety, the raven, with a triumphant caw, launched into the air, escaping the lion's clutches. It flew away, leaving behind a dream filled with bravery, friendship, and the adrenaline of a daring rescue.

Action & Adventure: The Knight of Wands is a card of action and adventure. It often represents a time when you feel motivated and ready to take on new challenges or adventures. This could be a physical journey or a metaphorical one, such as starting a new project or pursuing a passion.

Impulsiveness & Quick Decisions: This card is also associated with impulsiveness and quick decisions. The Knight of Wands doesn't wait around - he acts quickly and goes after what he wants. However, this can also lead to acting too hastily and failing to think things through.

Passion & Enthusiasm: The Knight of Wands is a passionate and enthusiastic character. This card suggests a time when you're driven by your desires, eager to pursue your passions, and full of energy.

Confidence & Charisma: This card also embodies the energy of confidence and charisma. It suggests a time when you're feeling bold, outgoing, and able to inspire others enthusiastically.

Change & Progress: On a deeper level, the Knight of Wands can signify change and progress. It's about breaking free from stagnation, embracing change, and moving forward.

QUEEN OF WANDS

The encountered within its dream a majestic raven queen who bore within her plumage a flame capable of illuminating the vast canvas of the night sky. This commanding figure embodied a boldness and self-assurance that transcended the domains of land and sky. Exuding an aura of regality, the queen invoked the spirits of the forest, enlisting their aid to manifest her aspirations. She held the power to shape the world. At the feet of the queen sat a rabbit, its presence signaling the promise of abundance and growth. It was a testament to the flourishing land under her reign, symbolizing fertility and proliferation. A graceful swan rested alongside the rabbit; its serene presence emanated an aura of harmony. Its silent pledge was to maintain the delicate balance of the queen's realm, fostering unity and peace.

Confidence & Self-Assuredness: The Queen of Wands is confident and self-assured. She knows her worth and is unafraid to express herself. This card can indicate a time of personal confidence and assertiveness, where you stand in your power.

Passion & Determination: This card brings passion and determination! The Queen of Wands pursues her goals with intense desire and dedication. She can indicate it is time for you to engage in a project, pursuit, or cause passionately.

Courage & Boldness: The Queen of Wands signifies courage and boldness. She is not afraid to take risks or face challenges head-on. This card can indicate when you are embracing your courage and stepping boldly toward your goals.

Independence & Self-Reliance: The Queen of Wands is also a symbol of independence and self-reliance. She is comfortable alone and doesn't need to rely on others for her success or happiness. This card can indicate when you are embracing your independence or depending on your resources to achieve your goals.

Optimism & Energy: This card embodies an energy of optimism and vibrancy. The Queen of Wands has a sunny disposition and looks at the world positively. This card can signify a time when you are feeling optimistic and energetic.

KING OF WANDS

The raven dreamt of an encounter between two unlikely conversationalists – another raven, appearing every bit the part of a king and a bear of considerable stature. The discourse between them was both fascinating and curious. The kingly raven, with a demeanor of royal authority, appeared to need assistance. It displayed a knack for diplomacy, lauding the bear for its renowned ability to foster cooperation and camaraderie. The raven's compliments were not mere flattery; they were strategic and astute, aimed at garnering the bear's support.The raven king exuded a charismatic presence that was hard to ignore. It knew just the right strings to pull, the precise words to utter to get the bear on its side. It was a master manipulator, guiding the conversation seamlessly toward the fruition of its plans. The spectacle the raven witnessed in its dream was a lesson in persuasion and strategy, a royal raven's cunning approach to achieving its objectives.

Leadership & Authority: The King of Wands is a natural-born leader. He is authoritative and ambitious, often taking charge in situations that require vision and leadership. This card can indicate the time has come for you to step into a leadership role or take control of a situation.

Vision & Boldness: This card is associated with vision and boldness. The King of Wands has a grand vision for the future and is unafraid to take risks to achieve his goals. Your situation may require acting boldly or pursuing a visionary goal.

Charisma & Inspiration: The King of Wands is charismatic and inspiring. He has a way with words and can motivate others to follow his lead. This card can indicate a time when you're inspiring others or being inspired by a charismatic figure.

Courage & Conviction: The King of Wands embodies courage and conviction. He is not afraid to stand up for what he believes in and is known for his strong convictions. This card can signify a time when you're standing up for your beliefs or showing courage in the face of adversity.

Creativity & Innovation: On a deeper level, the King of Wands signifies creativity and innovation. He embodies the entrepreneurial spirit, often blazing new trails and creating innovative solutions to problems.

ACE OF CUPS

In its dreams, the raven found itself by a tranquil lake, a haven of serenity and peace. The surrounding air was imbued with a sweet, gentle fragrance, giving the impression of a loving embrace extended by the mystical spirits of the forest. Upon the mirrored surface of the lake, a spectacle unfolded. A claw, possessing an enigmatic grace, ascended from the depths, clasping a lush lotus of breathtaking beauty. The unexpected yet utterly captivating sight held the raven's attention. The longer it gazed, the more a profound sense of happiness suffused through the raven, flowing from the crown of its head down to the tips of its feathers. The dreamlike encounter with the enigmatic claw and the radiant lotus was a harmonious convergence of awe and bliss, leaving the raven feeling open-hearted and emotionally fulfilled.

Love & Compassion: The Ace of Cups often signifies the beginning of a new, loving relationship. This could be a romantic relationship but can also refer to a new friendship or a deepening bond in an existing relationship.
Emotional Fulfillment & Happiness: This card represents fulfillment, joy, and contentment. It suggests a time of happiness and satisfaction, particularly in your emotional and spiritual dimensions.
Intuition & Inner Feelings: The Ace of Cups relates to intuition and inner feelings. It often shows up when you are more open to your subconscious and emotions. It encourages you to trust your intuition and to follow where it leads.

Creativity & Inspiration: Like other Aces, the Ace of Cups can signify a new creative venture or a surge of inspiration. However, in this case, the creative process will likely be particularly connected to your emotions or spiritual experience.

Spiritual Abundance & Healing: On a spiritual level, the Ace of Cups represents spiritual abundance and healing. It could signify the beginning of a spiritual journey or deep healing on an emotional or spiritual level.

TWO OF CUPS

In its slumber, the raven found itself beside an enchanting coastal lake, a mesmerizing blend of fresh and salty scents wafting through the air. Within the dream, it was engaged in its usual routine of catching fish when an unexpected figure appeared - a seagull. Under usual circumstances, the raven would have bristled at the newcomer's presence, instinctively guarding its food and territory. However, in this dream, an unusual affinity pulsed between the raven and the seagull, replacing the expected rivalry. In the tranquil corners of this vision, the two birds discovered a unique harmony. They collaborated in their fishing endeavors and warded off potential interlopers. It was a realm where a symbiotic partnership replaced competitive instincts. Upon awakening, the raven was wrapped in thoughtful contemplation, its dream still echoing. Perhaps, it mused, seagulls weren't adversaries to be battled but potential allies to be befriended. This altered perspective, a gift from its dream, added a new depth to the raven's understanding of its world.

Mutual Attraction and Connection: The Two of Cups brings mutual attraction between two people. This card often comes up when there's a strong connection, possibly a new relationship or friendship.

Partnership: This card may also signify a personal or professional collaboration is at the forefront. It's about working together, mutual respect, and balance. The partnership doesn't necessarily have to be romantic; it could be a close friendship, a business partnership, or a close collaboration.

Unity: The Two of Cups often signifies unity. It speaks to the harmony and emotional bond that two people can share, and it represents the beauty of mutual understanding and shared goals or values.

Love and Harmony: At its core, the Two of Cups offers love, peace, and harmony. It suggests a balanced relationship where individuals give and take equally, supporting each other's growth.

Commitment: Your situation may require a commitment or an agreement, such as an engagement or marriage, a business contract, or a verbal agreement between friends.

THREE OF CUPS

In its dream, the raven found itself amidst the desolation of a barren desert alongside two of its bird companions. The desolate landscape bore testimony to a prolonged dearth of rainfall that could easily span a few years. A shared understanding passed between the feathered trio as they turned their gaze skywards.

With determination kindled in their hearts, the ravens ascended to the heavens, their sharp beaks the chosen tools for an improbable task. As they punctured a solitary, dense, dark cloud, it responded by releasing a stream of long-awaited water. The arid ground drank greedily, quenching its thirst. In no time, the ravens found themselves basking in the downpour, their successful endeavor inviting a celebration under the cascading rain.

Celebration: The Three of Cups is typically associated with celebration or rejoicing. This could be related to a notable life event, such as a wedding, birth, graduation, or achievement, or it could denote a reason to gather and celebrate.

Friendship: This card often signifies strong bonds of friendship and camaraderie. It represents the joy, support, and companionship that come from social connections and shared experiences.

Collaboration: The Three of Cups can also denote successful collaboration or teamwork, often in a joyful or harmonious environment. This could be a successful work project or any scenario where working together with others leads to positive outcomes.

Community: Three of Cups directs your attention to community and belonging. It points to the strength and support found in these relationships and the sense of unity that can arise when people come together.

Joy and Gratitude: The Three of Cups reminds you to enjoy life's pleasures, give thanks, and celebrate your blessings.

FOUR OF CUPS

In its slumber, the raven found itself in solitude on the edge of a tranquil pond. This isolation was not a cause for distress; instead, it was a state the raven relished. An accidental glance at the pond revealed its mirror image and the raven was instantly captivated. It was so deeply engrossed in its reflection that it overlooked a morning glory vine entangling its leg. Despite the encroaching vine, the raven remained unmoved and uninterested in everything but its mirrored self. The vine continued to grow, tethering the raven closer to the Earth. All the while, unnoticed by the raven, a magnificent rose bloomed at its back, adding beauty to the scene that the captivated bird ignored. The vine grew unabated, enveloping the raven more and more, drawing it closer to the ground. Yet, the raven remained oblivious, fixated solely on its reflection. Finally, the raven awoke, startled. Stretching its wings wide, it relished the freedom of movement.

Dissatisfaction: The Four of Cups often appears when feeling dissatisfied or bored may impact your situation. You may feel unfulfilled by your current circumstances or disinterested in the opportunities presented to you.

Contemplation: A difficult situation might benefit from withdrawing from your external circumstances to reassess and reflect on your needs and desires.

Need for Self-Care: If you're feeling overwhelmed, uninterested, or disconnected, it might be time to prioritize self-care and replenish your emotional energy.

Missed Opportunities: The Four of Cups can suggest that you're so focused on your thoughts and feelings that you're missing out on potential opportunities. You might be so caught up in introspection that you ca unable see the opportunities or gifts being offered to you.

Apathy: The energy of this card can sometimes indicate apathy or a lack of motivation. This might be a result of feeling emotionally drained, or it could be that you're just feeling uninspired by the options available to you.

FIVE OF CUPS

The raven dreamt of a maternal raven had endured the heart-wrenching loss of four of her five offspring. Engulfed by her sorrow, her mournful cries echoed long and hard, the depth of her despair stirring the waters into a vortex that held the lifeless bodies of her offspring in an endless, sorrowful dance. Her heart was so entrenched in her grief that she couldn't divert her attention to the lone surviving fledgling. This last fledgling, perched precariously on the perimeter of her mother's tear-filled world, required the warmth of affection and support to grow and flourish. Yet, it stood ignored, as its mother was entangled in a web of grief, her focus unwavering from her loss.

Loss and Grief: The Five of Cups carries an energy of loss and the associated grief. This could result from a relationship breakup, losing a loved one, a missed opportunity, or any other significant loss.

Disappointment: This card suggests experiencing significant disappointment may be impacting your decisions. It could be that something you had high hopes for didn't turn out as expected, leaving you feeling disheartened.

Regret and Guilt: The Five of Cups may point to regret or guilt. You might be dwelling on past actions and their consequences, finding it hard to let go of what has happened.

Focus on the Negative: The Five of Cups often suggests a tendency to focus on the negative and overlook the positive. You might be so focused on what you've lost that you fail to recognize what you still have.

Need for Forgiveness: This card may appear if your situation would benefit from offering forgiveness. This might be forgiving someone else, but often it's about forgiving yourself. It's a reminder not to dwell on past mistakes but to learn from them and move forward.

SIX OF CUPS

Returning to the familiar landscapes of its youthful days, the raven dreamt of a tranquil lake. At the heart of this serene waterbody was a blooming lotus of exceptional size, its magnificence surpassing anything the raven had seen before. Dragonflies pirouetted in the air, their aerial ballet adding to the lake's peace and charm. The raven was bathed in a dual sense of serenity and youthful awe, captivated by the beautiful spectacle before it. Soon, the tranquil scene was graced by the appearance of an elegant swan trailed by a procession of six young ones. The sight ignited the raven's memory, kindling the embers of its past. As if transported by a time capsule, the raven was instantly swept back to the days of its youth, reliving those carefree, sun-drenched afternoons of yesteryears.

Nostalgia and Past Memories: The Six of Cups often represents a journey into the past, filled with nostalgic memories. It could signify revisiting old memories, possibly from childhood, and reminiscing about the "good old days."

Innocence: This card carries the energy of innocence and the pure joy of childhood. It's about remembering the simplicity, playfulness, and carefree nature of being a child.

Reunion or Reconnection: The Six of Cups can signify a reunion or reconnection with someone from your past. This might be an old friend or family member. This reconnection may bring a sense of joy and nostalgia.

Healing: This card often indicates a time of emotional healing. By reflecting on the past, you can see how far you've come and heal old emotional wounds.

SEVEN OF CUPS

In its dream, the raven envisioned seven shining crystals suspended in the starry canvas of the night sky. Each shimmering jewel was a container, safeguarding the raven's desires and apprehensions. The spectacle mesmerized the bird, its focus unwavering from the celestial display as it scrutinized each crystalline entity, mulling over the boundless possibilities they represented. As the nocturnal hours gradually wore on, an unsuspecting, plump caterpillar meandered onto the raven's foot.

Under normal circumstances, such an error would have spelled doom for the delectable morsel; however, this night was an exception. Immersed in the enticing fantasies the crystals offered, the raven remained oblivious to the easy prey within its reach. It permitted its mind to journey farther away from the mundane reality, beckoned by a realm of more captivating illusions.

Options and Choices: The Seven of Cups often represents many options and choices. It can indicate that you're faced with several opportunities and must make a decision.

Illusion and Fantasy: With a world of possibilities, not all options are grounded in reality! Some may be illusions or fantasies, and there's a need to discern between what's real and what's not. This card may appear when you risk procrastinating on something important because of being caught up in a fantasy.

Dreams and Desires: The Seven of Cups can symbolize the exploration of personal dreams and desires. It's about envisioning the possibilities and what could be. Dream big - but remember, a dream without action is just a fantasy!

Confusion: With so many choices, this card can also indicate your situation may suffer due to feeling confused or overwhelmed. It can suggest that it's challenging to decide due to unclear thoughts or emotions.

EIGHT OF CUPS

In its slumber, the raven found itself perched upon the bare spine of a cow, sun-bleached to immaculate purity. Although beautiful and peaceful, the situation stirred the raven with a lingering discontent. Its gaze wandered across the barren expanse of the desert, eventually landing on a lush meadow teeming with life. This verdant sight sparked a realization within the raven — it was indeed time for a transformation.

Transition and Change: The Eight of Cups often symbolizes a time of transition or change. It's about leaving behind what no longer serves you and moving on to something more meaningful.

Emotional Discontent: This card often appears when you feel discontent or disillusioned with your current situation. You might realize that something in your life is not bringing the satisfaction it once did.

Personal Quest: The Eight of Cups can represent a personal journey or quest for deeper meaning or fulfillment. This journey often involves emotional or spiritual growth.

Letting Go: This card carries the energy of release and letting go. It signifies the need to detach from something or someone to move forward emotionally.

Search for Truth: The Eight of Cups can indicate a deep search for truth or purpose. You may be trying to understand your emotions and motivations more deeply.

NINE OF CUPS

In its dream, the raven was nestled on a branch amidst a vibrant garden, a haven where all it could ever yearn for was within its grasp. Pride surged through its veins, pulsating with each heartbeat. As the dream unfolded, its tail began to transform, blooming into the glorious, flowing plumage characteristic of a peacock. The burgeoning pride enveloped the raven, making it yearn for the dream's perpetual continuation. The vestiges of contentment and gratitude persisted upon awakening. inspiring the bird to explore unexplored paths toward recapturing that feeling of having its wishes fulfilled in reality.

Wishes Fulfilled: The Nine of Cups often represents fulfilled wishes or desires. It's a card of satisfaction and contentment, suggesting that you will likely achieve what you desire.

Contentment and Satisfaction: This card represents emotional and material satisfaction. It suggests a time of happiness, pleasure, and enjoyment in life's comforts.

Gratitude: The Nine of Cups carries the energy of gratitude. It reminds us to appreciate and express thanks for our blessings.

Comfort: This card often represents a comfortable and pleasurable lifestyle. It can signify indulgence, enjoyment of life's luxuries, and self-satisfaction.

TEN OF CUPS

The raven envisioned a pair of majestic companions, perfectly aligned in symmetry. Their beaks interlocked to form a sturdy bridge, providing the woodland creatures a safe passage across a vast ravine. Within their beak's clasp, roots from a colossal communal tree reached into the water below, siphoning life-sustaining nourishment. This cyclic exchange kept the tree vibrant and lush, shaping a sanctuary of comfort and protection amidst the wilderness.

Emotional Fulfillment: The Ten of Cups often symbolizes complete emotional fulfillment and happiness. It's a card of joy, harmony, and contentment in your relationships, often within the family or home environment.

Harmony and Alignment: This card signifies harmony and alignment in relationships and family matters. It often indicates peaceful relationships and mutual respect among family members or close friends.

Happiness and Joy: The Ten of Cups represents ultimate happiness and joy. It's about enjoying the love and blessings in your life to the fullest.

Perfect Balance: The Ten of Cups signifies a perfect balance of love, friendship, family, and joy. It indicates that all aspects of your emotional life are in harmony.

Completion: The Ten of Cups suggests a joyous culmination and a sense of completion in your emotional life.

PAGE OF CUPS

In its dreams, the raven found itself as a mentor to an inquisitive young fox. Brimming with eagerness, the fox was keen to plunge into new experiences and engage with any creature willing to accompany it on its adventures. The raven's task was to embody the fox's internal compass of wisdom, acting as a guardian for the zealous youngster. Upon awakening, the raven mulled over the fox's many escapades and the idea that openness and creativity could pave the way to a life brimming with infinite possibilities.

Intuition & Inner Voice: The Page of Cups often represents a period where you're starting to listen to your intuition and your inner voice. It encourages you to trust your instincts and be open to what your subconscious is trying to tell you.

Opportunities & Surprises: This card can signify the arrival of unexpected opportunities or surprises, especially in emotional or spiritual growth. It may be a new relationship, a reconciliation, or a creative option that stirs your emotions.

Creativity & Imagination: The Page of Cups is associated with creativity and imagination. It suggests a period where you explore your creative side, tap into your imagination, or start a new creative project.

Curiosity & Openness: This card represents curiosity and openness. It's about being open to new experiences, exploring your feelings, and having a sense of wonder about the world around you.

Emotional Vulnerability & Innocence: On a deeper level, the Page of Cups may suggest a time of emotional vulnerability or innocence. It's about wearing your heart on your sleeve, expressing your emotions freely, and experiencing the highs and lows of emotional life.

KNIGHT OF CUPS

The raven succumbed to sleep, cloaked in sorrow and solitude. However, in its dream, it found solace nestled within the protective wing of an enormous, vibrant pink flamingo. The gentle, flamboyant feathers stirred an unexpected joy within the raven, driving away its sad thoughts. A wave of love engulfed the raven, dispelling the day's grief like mist before the morning sun. A renewed sense of self-assurance began to kindle within its heart. The dream dissolved just as the raven was settling into the comfort of this newfound bond. Even though the end of the dream brought a twinge of sadness, the raven deeply felt that such happiness was attainable once more.

Romance & Charm: The Knight of Cups is often associated with romance. They are the classic romantic Knight in shining armor, ready to sweep you off your feet. This card may indicate the presence of a romantic proposal or invitation or a person who embodies these qualities. Be aware, however, that the Knight of Cups can be a flake and, although they may sweep you off your feet, may become distracted or lack follow-through.

Idealism & Imagination: This card represents idealism and imagination. It suggests a time when you are allowing yourself to dream, to imagine the possibilities, and to approach the world with a sense of wonder.

Emotion & Intuition: The Knight of Cups is deeply connected to their emotions and intuition, following their heart and trusting their inner feelings. This card suggests a time when you are exploring your emotions, allowing them to guide your decisions. The Knight of Cups feels deeply and risks falling into the trap of brooding.

Creativity & Inspiration: The Knight of Cups can signify a period of creative inspiration. The Knight brings messages of artistic projects, creative inspiration, or new phases in your artistic expression.

Diplomacy & Grace: On a social level, this Knight knows how to navigate social situations with diplomacy and grace. They are tactful, diplomatic, and able to handle conflicts in a way that respects everyone's feelings.

QUEEN OF CUPS

Beneath the moon's silver glow, the queen of ravens dreamed of a transformative journey. Its jet-black plumage seamlessly morphed into glossy, grey fur, assuming the enchanting form of a selkie. It plunged into the invigorating chill of the ocean, a newfound liberty blossoming with its dual existence. The raven discovered a novel existence beneath the waves, building an unprecedented bridge between the aerial realms and the aquatic abyss. Submerged, the raven felt a profound connection to the Earth's energy. This pulsating rhythm connected it to the emotions of the marine creatures it met, revealing a deeper, more empathetic layer of existence.

Intuition & Inner Wisdom: The Queen of Cups is profoundly intuitive and connected with her inner wisdom. She trusts her gut feelings and pays attention to her dreams. This card can signify when you're tapping into your intuition or inner wisdom.

Emotional Awareness & Sensitivity: This card is associated with emotional awareness and sensitivity. The Queen of Cups is aware of her own emotions and the emotions of others. She is empathetic and understanding, capable of providing emotional support.

Compassion & Empathy: The Queen of Cups embodies compassion and empathy. She is a nurturing figure, caring for others with a deep sense of understanding and love. This card can indicate you're acting as a caretaker or providing emotional support to someone else.

Creativity & Imagination: The Queen of Cups also represents creativity and imagination. She has a rich inner life and often expresses her feelings through creative or artistic outlets. This card can signify when you're exploring your creative side or using creativity to work through emotions.

Mystery & The Unconscious: The Queen of Cups may represent the mysterious and unconscious aspects of the self. She often appears when there is a need to pay attention to dreams, unconscious thoughts, or symbols that can provide insight into your emotional life.

KING OF CUPS

In its dreamscape, the raven envisioned a colossal wave. This monstrous surge loomed menacingly over the sea creatures and a humble fishing vessel, threatening to hurl them onto the unforgiving land. Just as doom seemed inevitable, the majestic raven king unfurled its mighty wings, splitting the towering wall of water and creating a haven of tranquility. This intervention allowed the marine dwellers to retreat to the secure depths of the ocean. The raven king then exerted a calming influence, gently soothing the tumultuous waters and gradually causing the formidable wave to withdraw, restoring peace to the once-threatened oceanic realm.

Emotional Balance & Maturity: The King of Cups is known for his emotional intelligence and maturity. He can balance his emotions and intellect to make wise decisions. This card may appear when you are being called to maintain emotional balance or demonstrate emotional maturity.

Compassion & Understanding: This card is associated with compassion and understanding. The King of Cups is empathetic, caring, and understanding. He listens to others and offers emotional support. This card may signify your time to provide or receive emotional support.

Diplomacy & Tact: The King of Cups is a diplomatic figure. He can navigate tricky situations with tact and understanding, often bringing peace and resolution to conflicts. This card may indicate a situation that requires diplomacy and tact.

Wisdom & Counsel: The King of Cups is often seen as a counselor or advisor, offering wise and empathetic guidance.

ACE OF SWORDS

In its slumber, the raven found itself in a garden teeming with delicate forget-me-nots, a potential cue to recall the dream upon awakening. From the sea of blossoms emerged a claw clutching a nest, cradling an owl. Abruptly, the raven's gaze shifted from terrestrial beauty to the celestial expanse, an immense vista that offered miles of unobstructed clarity. As swiftly as it ascended, its perspective returned to the earthly domain. Throughout this dream, the raven gained a profound understanding of the intricate bond weaving together the realms of the Earth and the sky.

Clarity & Insight: The Ace of Swords often signifies a moment of clarity or insight. It suggests a time when the fog is lifting, and you can see the truth of a situation more clearly.

New Ideas & Breakthroughs: This card represents new ideas, breakthroughs, and fresh ways of thinking. It can suggest that you're in the early stages of a new project or are about to have a significant breakthrough in your thoughts or understanding.

Truth & Justice: The Ace of Swords is also connected with the concepts of truth and justice. It encourages you to see the truth, speak your truth, and stand up for what is right and fair.

Mental Power & Assertiveness: This card symbolizes mental power and assertiveness. It suggests overcoming confusion, overcoming obstacles, and asserting your ideas and intentions.

Victory & Success: On some level, the Ace of Swords can indicate victory or success, especially after a struggle. It's a card of triumph and achievement through clear vision, mental focus, and determination.

TWO OF SWORDS

In its dream, the raven found itself in the grip of a snake's mouth, a predator ready to seal its fate swiftly. Nevertheless, the raven mustered the strength to fend off the snake's razor-sharp fangs. Hovering above the raven, a cage materialized; the raven watched as its heart separated from its body, securing itself within the cage, as if placed under some divine protection. Then, an influx of petite white moths descended upon the raven's head, their delicate wings obscuring its view of the snake, which instilled an uncertainty about its subsequent action. However, the raven perceived that maintaining its position could at least evade the impending threat of being consumed.

Indecision and Stalemate: The Two of Swords often represents a situation where you're caught between two choices, resulting in delay or a stalemate. You may feel stuck, unable to move forward until a decision is made.

Balance and Duality: This card often signifies balance and duality. It suggests a need to balance your mind and heart to make a decision, or it might represent a situation where two opposing forces are in balance but locked in a stalemate.

Denial or Avoidance: The Two of Swords may suggest your situation is being impacted due to avoidance or denying the reality of a problem. You might be refusing to acknowledge the truth or avoiding making a tough decision.

THREE OF SWORDS

Roused from an intensely vivid dream, the raven was left trembling; she pondered whether the dream held prophetic implications—it had felt so undeniably real. She reflected on the chilling scenario. Despite being keenly aware, the raven could feel the piercing prongs of a pitchfork impaling her body, her heart throbbing with the raw torment of the inflicted wound. Amid her agony, she perceived a familiar pull, only to witness her mate—her life's companion—feasting on her flesh. Beneath her, she noticed her sister indulging in her spilled life essence. The scene was a confounding paradox—where was the funeral rite? Why were they reveling in this grim demise rather than mourning it?

Heartbreak and Emotional Pain: The Three of Swords is often associated with heartbreak, sorrow, and emotional pain. This card often appears when there is the potential for you to go through a difficult emotional period, such as a breakup or a betrayal.

Separation and Loss: This card can also signify separation or loss. This could be a relationship ending, losing a loved one, or any other significant loss.

Truth and Clarity: The Three of Swords can also bring clarity and truth despite the painful connotations. Your situation may benefit from acknowledging the pain or reality, as this will be the first step towards healing and moving forward.

Release and Healing: The Three of Swords, sometimes depending on the circumstances, may symbolize the need for emotional release. It's a reminder that it's okay to grieve, to feel your emotions fully, and to allow the healing process to unfold.

FOUR OF SWORDS

In its dreamscape, the raven grappled with deep mental and physical fatigue. A concept was swirling within its mind, but the relentless cacophony around it rendered contemplation almost impossible. Within this dreamland, the raven spied a rabbit surfacing from a burrow. Seizing the opportunity when all seemed secure, the bird hopped down into the haven of the warren. At long last, tranquility, the bird mused. Enveloped by the comforting, stabilizing ambiance of the soil and roots, the raven found serenity. For the first time, it could truly discern the internal messages that had long been striving to surface.

Rest and Recuperation: The Four of Swords often symbolizes a period of rest and recovery that will benefit a situation. It suggests a need to take time out to rejuvenate and restore your energy, especially if you've been under a lot of stress.

Contemplation and Reflection: This card can also signify a time for contemplation and reflection. It's about taking a break from your usual routine to reflect on your life and gain a new perspective.

Preparation: The Four of Swords can also indicate a period of preparation. You might be resting and gathering your strength in preparation for a future challenge or task.

Solitude: In some cases, this card suggests solitude. You might need some alone time to sort through your thoughts and feelings.

FIVE OF SWORDS

In its dream, the raven chanced upon an idyllic location teeming with fish. After successfully procuring a bounty of five, the bird decided it was time to feast. Suddenly, an unforeseen force toppled the raven. With a weight pressing down on it and unable to lift its head, the bird felt an ominous, low growl—it was a panther. The formidable beast pinned the bird firmly to the ground, yet it kept its claws sheathed. The raven understood that the panther hadn't appeared to claim its life or steal its hard-earned catch. Instead, it was there to impart a stark reminder that it held the power to do so, should it wish.

Conflict and Defeat: The Five of Swords often symbolizes conflict, tension, and defeat. It might appear when you're involved in a dispute or facing opposition or challenges. Someone may be acting like a bully.
Win at All Costs: This card indicates a "win at all costs" mentality. It suggests that you might be so focused on winning or being right that you're neglecting the feelings or needs of others. On the flip side, you may be the one who is being pushed aside by another's hunger for success.
Tension and Disagreement: The Five of Swords can represent tension, disagreements, and conflict. It suggests a lack of harmony and can indicate arguments or conflicts of interest.
Re-evaluating: Your situation may benefit from re-evaluating your situation or approach. If your current strategy leads to conflict or loss, it might be time to reconsider your actions and change your tactics.

SIX OF SWORDS

After an arduous day, punctuated by a confrontation with a rival bird that forced the raven to consider new refuge, a dream began to weave itself as the raven sought rest. In this dream, the raven, unable to fly, was aboard a boat, its wing and eye badly injured. Despite the ominous darkness of the sea, the bird was guided by the soft glow of a lantern. Occupying the boat was a heart, radiating an aura of love and offering emotional aid during its voyage. Emerging from the water were six gleaming needles. These symbols imbued the raven with a sense of tranquility, instilling the reassurance that even though it was currently adrift, the promise of healing and restoration awaited.

Transition and Change: The Six of Swords represents a period of transition or change. It suggests moving from a place of turbulence to calmer waters, indicating progress and improvements.

Moving On: This card represents moving on, which often includes leaving behind something that no longer serves you or is harmful. It might be a relationship, a job, or old belief patterns.

Healing Journey: The Six of Swords can also signify a healing journey. This could be emotional, mental, or physical healing, often following difficulty or hardship.

Safe Passage: The card suggests you're being guided or protected during this transition period. You're not alone in this journey; support is available, whether physical or spiritual.

SEVEN OF SWORDS

The raven revealed to the fox its fatigue of consistently dividing its meals with its mate, voicing a desire to relish a solo feast fit for royalty for once. The cunning fox listened with rapt attention, echoing that the raven indeed deserved to savor the bountiful fish all by itself. Serving as a pillar of support, the fox proposed an intriguing solution; the raven could temporarily confine its mate within a box, allowing it to enjoy its meal undisturbed, while its partner remained oblivious in the darkness. The raven deemed this an exceptional plan, extending gratitude to its newfound confidant. Later that afternoon, with a sense of triumphant anticipation, the raven set the trap, relishing the thought of a solitary fish feast. Meanwhile, the fox loitered inconspicuously in the vicinity, keenly awaiting the moment the box would close. Before the raven could taste its first morsel of fish, the fox sprang into action! The fox leisurely savored the raven and the fish before carrying the 'to-go' box home, reserved for a delightful midnight treat.

Strategy and Deception: The Seven of Swords often represents strategic thinking but can also suggest deception or manipulative behavior. You may need to be strategic in your approach to a situation, or someone might need to be more honest with you.

Stealth and Secret Plans: This card can signify operating secretly or working behind the scenes to achieve a goal. It can suggest that subtlety and stealth are required rather than confronting a situation directly.

Independence: The Seven of Swords can also suggest a desire to be independent or do things your way. It might indicate a need to rely on your resources or abilities rather than those of others.

Taking Risks: In some cases, this card can indicate taking risks. It might suggest that you're pushing the boundaries or taking a chance, but with the risk of negative consequences if discovered.

EIGHT OF SWORDS

In its dream, the raven observed its own actions as though viewing a film on a screen. Donning a mask, its dream self romped through a stunning, aromatic garden. The atmosphere was thick with mist and drifting pollen, yet the masked raven was oblivious, protected by its vibrant red mask. The spectacle continued as the visually impaired raven ensnared a mouse, seemingly immersed in the delightful garden scenario. As the fog gradually dissipated, the appearance of the idyllic garden began to alter, yet the sightless raven remained ignorant of the shifting environment. The observing raven started questioning its own perceptions — could it, too, be blind to potential threats? Had it become so complacent that it risked falling into a trap?

Restriction and Confusion: The Eight of Swords often represents feelings of restriction, confusion, or entrapment. It suggests that you may feel trapped or limited, but these feelings are often self-imposed or due to a lack of perspective.

Self-limitation: This card may appear when self-limiting beliefs or thoughts restrict progress. It's about feeling stuck, but your fears or insecurities often hold you back, rather than external circumstances.

Victim Mentality: The Eight of Swords can indicate a victim mentality. It might suggest that you're allowing yourself to be controlled by circumstances or other people rather than asserting your power.

Need for Release: Your situation will benefit from releasing self-imposed restrictions. A new perspective or freeing yourself from negative thinking can provide a way out of the current situation.

NINE OF SWORDS

The raven wakened to find itself immersed in a dream laden with unease. Its body was contorted and inverted, an unsettling sight. No matter which direction the raven endeavored to navigate, piercing thorns cruelly penetrated its feathers, reaching its tender skin. Safeguarding the closed box was a formidable battalion of hornets, their relentless, discordant buzzing contributing to the disoriented raven's distress. The raven woke from this lucid dream feeling shaken. Something was calling its attention!

Anxiety and Fear: The Nine of Swords often represents anxiety, worry, or fear. It can indicate that you're situation is being impacted by feeling overwhelmed by negative thoughts or fears, possibly leading to insomnia or nightmares.

Mental Anguish: This card symbolizes mental distress or anguish. It suggests a period of intense worry or stress that may be disproportionate to the actual problem or situation.

Guilt or Regret: The Nine of Swords can also represent feelings of guilt or regret. You may be dwelling on past mistakes or worrying about things that have not yet happened.

Need for Help: This card often serves as a sign that you may need to seek help to deal with your worries or fears. Talking to someone about your problems could bring relief or a solution and, as a result, promote positive progress.

TEN OF SWORDS

In its dream, the raven found itself journeying through an ominous forest alongside its mate when they inadvertently encountered a hostile swarm of yellow jackets. Aware that the aggressive swarm could not pursue both birds simultaneously, the raven's mate proposed they diverge paths. At this moment, the raven discerned its mate's foresight. The path they had embarked upon was fraught with danger, a fact its mate knew all too well, and it had premeditated an escape route well before this lethal encounter.

Painful Endings: The Ten of Swords represents a painful ending or a deep wound. This could be a betrayal, a disappointment, or a harsh reality that needs to be confronted.

Dramatic Change: This card suggests a dramatic change or upheaval. It is often associated with the end of a cycle or phase in your life. This end can be painful but clears the way for a new beginning.

Release and Surrender: To progress, you may need to let go and accept the current situation rather than fighting against it.

Rebirth: Despite its seemingly negative connotations, the Ten of Swords often carries the promise of rebirth. It's the dawn after the darkest hour, hinting at the start of a new, more positive cycle.

Victim Mentality: You may need to consider if your situation is stagnant or stuck due to settling into the role of the victim.

PAGE OF SWORDS

In its dream, the raven imagined itself as a fledgling, teetering on the precipice of mastering the art of flight. Observing swallows trace graceful arcs through the sky, swooping around the trees, filled the enthusiastic young bird with excitement. It vividly shared its envisioning of a boundless, liberating life with all willing to listen. Once the bird felt at home amid the expanse of the sky, it bravely urged the other fledglings to accompany it, encouraging them to claim their own freedom.

Curiosity & Exploration: The Page of Swords often signifies a period of exploration and curiosity. It represents a thirst for knowledge and a desire to uncover the truth.

New Ideas & Plans: This card is about new ideas and plans, particularly those that involve communication, intellectual pursuits, or the search for truth. It suggests a time when you are thinking clearly, making new plans, and excited by new ideas.

Communication & Expression: The Page of Swords is associated with clear communication and expressing thoughts. It indicates that you might enter a phase where effective communication, particularly of new ideas or complex concepts, will be necessary.

Mental Energy & Alertness: This card symbolizes mental energy and alertness. It suggests a time when you are mentally agile and prepared, ready to tackle any intellectual or communicative challenges that come your way. Honesty & Truth: On a deeper level, the Page of Swords is about honesty and truth. It encourages you to communicate honestly, seek the truth, and stand up for what you believe is right.

KNIGHT OF SWORDS

The raven dreamt of a daring heist executed by an audacious young raccoon. The raccoon meticulously plotted the swift abduction of a fledgling Stellar Jay, leaving no stone unturned, save for overlooking one crucial detail - the vigilant father Stellar Jay was in close proximity to the nest. The resolute father Jay, recognizing the imminent danger, descended from the sky with unmatched speed and determination. Faced with this formidable adversary, the raccoon realized there was only one viable option left - to return the baby and beat a hasty retreat.

Action & Determination: The Knight of Swords is a card of action and determination. It often represents a time when you're charging ahead, determined to achieve your goals no matter what stands in your way.

Directness & Assertiveness: This card is associated with directness and assertiveness. The Knight of Swords doesn't hold back – he speaks his mind and isn't afraid to confront issues head-on.

Quick Thinking & Intellect: The Knight of Swords is also a symbol of quick thinking and intellect. This card suggests when you're making quick decisions, thinking on your feet, and using your intellect to navigate complex situations.

Courage & Ambition: This card represents courage and ambition. It signifies a time when you're feeling brave, ambitious, and ready to take on any challenges that come your way.

Conflict & Confrontation: On a more challenging note, the Knight of Swords can also represent conflict or confrontation. He can indicate when you need to defend your ideas or confront others.

QUEEN OF SWORDS

In its dream, the raven envisioned a majestic queen presiding from a perch overlooking a vast labyrinth. Nestled within the towering walls of the intricate maze thrived life in all its varied forms. The queen possessed an uncanny ability to discern those who were trapped and those poised for success. Her vision extended beyond the immediate, capable of foreseeing the next move, the path ahead, and the hurdles obstructing progress. From her elevated vantage point, she skillfully guided those who sought her counsel, charting the most effective course forward.

Clarity & Communication: The Queen of Swords is a clear thinker and articulate speaker. She values truth and communicates her thoughts and ideas with clarity and precision. This card can indicate a situation that will benefit from speaking your truth or seeking clarity in your thoughts and ideas.

Independence & Self-reliance: This card is strongly associated with independence and self-reliance. The Queen of Swords is a lone figure, often indicating a period of solitude or independence. She can care for herself and relies on her wisdom to make decisions.

Wisdom & Life Experience: The Queen of Swords embodies wisdom from life experience. She has faced many challenges and used these experiences to grow and develop a deep understanding of life. This card can signify a time when you are drawing on your own life experiences to navigate a situation.

Objective Judgement & Rationality: This card represents objectivity and rationality. The Queen of Swords is a logical thinker who makes decisions based on facts rather than emotions. This card can indicate when you're being called to decide objectively or impartially.

Courage & Honesty: On a deeper level, the Queen of Swords signifies courage and honesty. She is not afraid to face the truth, no matter how uncomfortable. This card can suggest you are confronting a difficult reality or facing a situation with bravery.

KING OF SWORDS

In its dream, the raven envisioned a formidable raven, assertively perched atop a gravestone and positioned before the bird were three symbolic hourglasses. The first represented the potential for resourcefulness, the second embodied emotions, and the third encapsulated clarity of thought. The raven, steadfast in its dedication to justice and fairness, meticulously determined the amount of time to be devoted to each domain, thereby ensuring a near-certain path to success.

Intellect & Clarity: The King of Swords is known for his intellect and clear thinking. He is analytical and logical, able to cut through confusion to get to the heart of the matter. This card can indicate when you rely on your intellect to solve problems or make decisions, you will find the best outcome.

Truth & Justice: This card is associated with truth and justice. The King of Swords values honesty and integrity and often symbolizes law, order, and fairness. This card can signify a situation where truth and justice are paramount.

Authority & Command: The King of Swords is an authoritative figure, respected for his wisdom and clear judgment. He is a leader who commands respect. This card may appear when you are stepping into a position of authority or need to assert your authority.

Decision Making & Strategy: The King of Swords is a strategist who makes decisions based on a clear understanding of the situation and long-term objectives. Your situation may require you to make strategic decisions or plan for the future.

Impartiality & Objectivity: The King of Swords also represents impartiality and objectivity. He can detach himself from emotional considerations to make fair and balanced decisions. This card can appear when you need to be objective or impartial.

ACE OF PENTACLES

The raven stirred awake from a dream, radiant with renewed enthusiasm. It dreamt of perching atop a cloud from where it beheld a grand spectacle. A mighty claw ascended through the mist, bearing a lush tree with fragrant blossoms. The tree's roots cascaded towards the Earth below, anchoring it in an embrace. Nestled in the claw was a nest cradling an egg on the brink of hatching. The dream was perfumed with the promise of hope and abundance. The raven felt invigorated, ready to embark on a new endeavor, certain that this prophetic dream was a harbinger of prosperous times ahead.

Opportunity & Potential: The Ace of Pentacles often signifies a new option on the horizon, especially in material or financial prospects. It's a card of potential and suggests that you are on the brink of starting something with promising growth prospects.

Prosperity & Abundance: This card represents prosperity and abundance. It suggests that you may be about to enter a period of financial security, success, or good fortune.

New Ventures & Projects: The Ace of Pentacles is often associated with beginning new ventures or projects, particularly those with potential for financial or material gain. It could be a new business, investment, or other financial opportunity.

Manifestation & Realization: The Ace of Pentacles is also about manifestation. It's about taking your ideas and making them real, turning your plans into action, and seeing tangible results.

Health & Well-Being: On a more personal level, the Ace of Pentacles can also signify a period of good health and physical well-being. It suggests a time of feeling grounded and secure in one's physical self.

TWO OF PENTACLES

In its dream, the raven found itself hungry. Abundance was within its reach, but it demanded resourcefulness. The raven deftly flicked the first pill bug into the air, where it reflexively curled into a tight sphere. With the precision of a practiced performer, the raven balanced the round bug on its wing. The raven had secured two meals by repeating the maneuver with a second pill bug. This clever act of foresight ensured it would be well-fed, even if a sudden turn of events rendered food scarce.

Balance and Adaptability: The Two of Pentacles often symbolizes the need for balance, especially regarding resources or responsibilities. It's about juggling multiple tasks, priorities, or commitments and trying to keep everything in balance.

Change and Flux: This card can signify change and flux, especially concerning financial or material matters. It might indicate fluctuations in income or expenses or changing circumstances that require flexibility.

Time Management: The Two of Pentacles often represents time management. Your situation may require balancing work and personal life or multiple responsibilities.

Decision: You may need to decide where to allocate your time or resources. You may need to determine which tasks or commitments are most important.

THREE OF PENTACLES

In its dream, the raven conceived a grand gesture of love for its mate – a distinct emblem etched onto their favorite tree in the forest. Seeking assistance from a friendly flicker, the raven relayed its imaginative concept. The flicker, with its fine-pointed beak, diligently set to work. In due time, a masterfully carved sculpture emerged from the tree bark, a testament to their shared affection and a pledge for a loving future together.

Teamwork and Collaboration: The Three of Pentacles often represents teamwork and collaboration. Working with others, each bringing unique skills, can help accomplish a common goal.

Appreciation: This card often denotes that others appreciate your work. It can signify gaining respect, recognition, or reward for your work or skills.

Planning and Implementation: This card may call your attention to a project's planning and implementation stages. It suggests the initial satisfaction of seeing your plans become a reality.

Skills and Expertise: The Three of Pentacles indicates mastery, suggesting that your skills are being recognized. Alternatively, relying on the expertise of others may be beneficial.

FOUR OF PENTACLES

The raven dreamt of an overwhelming fear that seagulls might exhaust the sea's bounty of fish. In its dream, it would industriously gather as many fish as it could bear, transporting them to a secret hideaway. Here, it would savor one fish while stockpiling the rest, apprehensive of an impending famine. Anxiety-stricken, the raven hovered near its secret stash, only daring to venture out momentarily to amass more fish.

The air became hot and humid. The raven embarked once again on its routine expedition to the shore. This time, however, the watchful seagulls had caught onto its scheme and barred it from the beach. Returning to its cache with a grumbling stomach, the raven was greeted by a putrid stench. Digging through the soil, it discovered its hoard of fish decaying.

The raven's dread of the seagulls exhausting the fish and its belief in the sea's limited supplies had spiraled into greed. Ironically, it was this very fear of scarcity that ultimately left the raven famished.

Security and Control: The Four of Pentacles often represents a desire for security and control, particularly regarding money and material possessions. It suggests holding on tightly to what you have out of fear of loss.

Possessiveness and Materialism: This card can signify possessiveness, greed, or materialism. It might suggest that being overly focused on material possessions or financial status impacts your situation.

Stability: The Four of Pentacles can symbolize stability and firm foundations. This could indicate financial stability or a stable position in life more generally.

Resistance to Change: You should consider whether there is resistance to change or a fear of instability. It can suggest being stuck in your comfort zone and fearful or resistant to venturing out.

FIVE OF PENTACLES

The raven jolted awake from a distressing dream. It found itself grounded on the frosty, snow-dusted ground while its wings remained ensnared in the tree branches above! The bird's initial attempts to retrieve its wings proved futile – leaping to dislodge them yielded no result; its calls for its mate echoed unanswered, and each effort to scramble up the tree was thwarted by relentless gravity. An overwhelming sense of despair settled over the raven as the prospect of a wingless existence took root. A bone-chilling cold crept up from the rapidly freezing ground, compounding its dread. As hope dwindled to a mere trace, an unexpected savior appeared—a tiny mouse clutching a needle and thread. The raven paused, wrestling with its thoughts. It might have to swallow its pride and beseech the minuscule creature to fetch its wings. But what if the mouse greeted its plea with mockery, given the raven had likely preyed on some of its kin in the past? Poised to voice its desperate request, the raven was abruptly awakened, left hanging in suspense about whether aid would have been extended.

Financial Loss and Hardship: The Five of Pentacles often represents financial loss, hardship, or poverty. It suggests a period of financial struggle or material insecurity.
Feeling Excluded or Unwanted: This card also symbolizes feeling left out in the cold, isolated, or excluded. This could be on a social, emotional, or spiritual level, in addition to or instead of financial hardship.
Health Concerns: The Five of Pentacles may relate to poor health or physical strain, particularly if it's leading to financial strain.
Hope: Despite its generally negative connotations, this card also conveys hope. It suggests that help is available, but you must be willing to ask for or accept it.

SIX OF PENTACLES

In its dream, the raven found itself in the harsh, relentless desert alongside its partner. Water was a fleeting memory, and the sweltering heat grew unbearable with each passing moment. A glance around revealed a stark panorama of bleached bones, the desert's grim trophies, sparking fear

In its dream, the raven found itself in the harsh, relentless desert alongside its partner. Water was a fleeting memory, and the sweltering heat grew unbearable with each passing moment. A glance around revealed a stark panorama of bleached bones, the desert's grim trophies, sparking fear about their impending fate in this desolate wasteland.

Suddenly, the silence was broken by a thunderous cry overhead. Before they could fully grasp the situation, a giant raven materialized, cascading a bounty of water and fish from a large bucket. Gratitude washed over them in waves, even as they wondered about the fate of the rabbits dotting the horizon. Was there something out there that would provide hope for these fellow wanderers?

Charity and Generosity: The Six of Pentacles often represents charity, generosity, and giving. It suggests a situation where wealth or resources are being shared, often from a place of abundance.

Reciprocity and Fairness: This card also symbolizes reciprocity and fairness. It can suggest a situation where resources are being balanced, or debts are being repaid.

Giving and Receiving: The Six of Pentacles embodies the flow of resources through giving and receiving. This card can also symbolize a gift, a grant, or a form of financial assistance.

Having / Not Having: The Six of Pentacles may direct your attention to your position within a situation. Do you have the resources to proceed with a plan, or are you dependent on someone with more resources?

SEVEN OF PENTACLES

In its dream, the raven devised a novel strategy; rather than idly waiting for the ocean to deposit fish upon the shore, it decided to take the matter into its own wings by setting traps in the bay. After a day's wait, the bird curiously submerged its head underwater to inspect its traps. While some had trapped fish, others had remained barren. Undeterred, the raven lifted the empty traps and relocated them to a different part of the bay. Another day rolled by, and once again, the raven dutifully surveyed its traps. The patient bird finally found the optimal locations for each trap, ensuring the maximum yield of fish.

Patience and Waiting: The Seven of Pentacles often represents patience and anticipation. It suggests a period of waiting for the results or rewards of your hard work.

Assessment and Reflection: This card suggests a moment of reflection or assessment. You may be reviewing your progress so far, contemplating the results of your efforts, or considering whether your current path aligns with your long-term goals.

Perseverance: The Seven of Pentacles suggests investing in your efforts, even if the results aren't immediately visible.

Harvest and Rewards: This card often denotes that you're nearing the stage where you can reap the fruits of your labor. However, it's crucial to have patience and not rush the process.

EIGHT OF PENTACLES

In its dream, the raven had ingeniously crafted a spear using sticks, vines, and a discarded piece of metal found near a campsite, significantly improving its fishing capabilities in the lake. Yet, in this dreamscape, the raven wasn't satisfied with the limitations of its short spear and embarked on a diligent journey to construct a more robust and elongated one capable of reaching the larger fish dwelling at the lake's depths.

Over time, coupled with extensive trial and error, the raven honed its spear-making craft to perfection and achieved its goal! The bird was brimming with energy and a newfound sense of capability upon awakening. The raven was eager to master a fresh skill in reality, imbued with the belief that success was indeed within its reach.

Dedication and Skill Development: The Eight of Pentacles often represents dedication, diligence, and attention to detail. It's about honing your skills, mastering your craft, and taking pride in your work.

Hard Work and Productivity: This card can also symbolize a period of hard work and high productivity. It suggests that you're committed to your tasks and putting in the effort to get the job done.

Apprenticeship and Learning: Your situation may benefit from an apprenticeship or learning. You might be learning a new skill, studying, or working under a mentor.

Perfectionism: The Eight of Pentacles may also signify perfectionism. While striving for excellence is a positive trait, avoiding being overly critical or setting unrealistic standards is essential.

NINE OF PENTACLES

During one slumber, the raven found itself immersed in a fantastical dream featuring an elegant peacock that had befriended a raven, providing it with a cozy nesting spot within an ornate wig. They would whittle away their afternoons, strolling through an expansive garden, basking in the enchanting scenery that enveloped them.

While the sophisticated peacock was entirely self-reliant, she occasionally beckoned the raven to pluck an apple from a nearby tree when hunger pangs hit. Confident in their bond, she knew the raven would select the most succulent fruit and swiftly return to its unique perch, ready to continue their peaceful saunter through the garden.

Abundance and Independence: The Nine of Pentacles represents a period of abundance, prosperity, and financial independence. Financial stability and self-sufficiency will enter your situation.

Enjoyment of the Finer Things: This card can symbolize enjoying the finer things in life, such as luxury, comfort, or a beautiful environment. It's about appreciating and enjoying what you have worked hard to achieve.

Confidence and Self-esteem: The Nine of Pentacles often represents a state of inner confidence and self-esteem. You are comfortable in your own skin and proud of your achievements.

Leisure and Solitude: Your situation may benefit from a period of leisure or solitude. You may enjoy time alone, nurturing yourself, or pursuing your interests.

TEN OF PENTACLES

In its dream, the raven discovered an impressively large pine cone, a potential seed for a future shelter that could be a haven for generations. The bird ferried this treasure to an optimal location, which it discerned would be most conducive to growth. With diligent work and anticipation of a prosperous future, the raven set about its task, confident that its investment of time and effort would reap substantial rewards in due course.

Wealth and Legacy: The Ten of Pentacles represents wealth, inheritance, and legacy. It suggests a period of financial security and stability, often built up over time and potentially extending to your family or the next generation.

Completion and Accomplishment: This card also symbolizes a sense of completion or accomplishment. You have achieved your goals and established a lasting foundation for your future.

Family and Home: The Ten of Pentacles can symbolize a happy and secure family life. It might suggest a family business, a secure home, or enjoying familial relationships.

Long-term Stability: This card represents long-term stability and financial security, as opposed to short-term gains. It often denotes investments, property, or other assets that will have long-lasting value.

PAGE OF PENTACLES

The raven stirred from an intriguing dream filling it with curiosity and a renewed zest for experimentation. It had dreamt of perching atop a snake in a perpetual cycle of consuming its own tail. In the center of this circle was a bright full moon. A carefree mouse circled the scene, indifferent to the lurking threat. Emblazoned within this cosmic loop, the raven saw a Trinacria symbol formed by a three-winged raven, a potent emblem of fertility and prosperity. The raven interpreted the sight as a divine affirmation, a hint of potential, and the promise of abundance. Emboldened by this revelation, the raven woke, ready to set its newfound plan into action, confident that success was within reach.

Opportunity & Potential: The Page of Pentacles often represents a new opportunity or potential, particularly related to your work, finances, or studies. It suggests a time when you're starting a new project, job, or course of study with many potentials.

Ambition & Desire: This card embodies the energy of ambition and desire. It's about setting your sights on a goal and being willing to work hard to achieve it.

Practicality & Responsibility: The Page of Pentacles also represents practicality and responsibility. It's about making practical plans, dealing with day-to-day responsibilities, and managing resources wisely.

Learning & Studying: The Page of Pentacles suggests your situation may benefit from studying, learning new skills, or seeking knowledge. It encourages you to remain curious, open-minded, and eager to learn.

Manifestation & Materialization: The Page of Pentacles is about the process of manifestation. It's about manifesting your dreams and ambitions in the physical world.

KNIGHT OF PENTACLES

In its dream, the raven traversed the vast forest atop an enormous elephant, their intended destination teasingly concealed from view. The raven, attracted by an intriguing spectacle off the beaten path, desired to diverge from the route and embark on an impromptu detour. Yet, the elephant, a creature of singular focus and resolve, stubbornly adhered to the planned route. The raven's pleas grew more insistent, its caws ringing through the forest in an attempt to steer their journey elsewhere, but the steadfast elephant remained undeterred. As such, their progression was a steady march forward, regardless of the raven's itch to investigate the captivating curiosities that dotted their surroundings.

Diligence & Patience: The Knight of Pentacles often represents a time of perseverance and patience. Unlike other Knights who are constantly in motion, the Knight of Pentacles is stationary, indicating dedication, focus, and an organized approach to achieving goals.

Responsibility & Hard Work: This card is associated with commitment and hard work. The Knight of Pentacles takes their duties seriously, and this card might suggest a time when you are committed to fulfilling your obligations and responsibilities.

Routine & Methodology: The Knight of Pentacles is also about routine and following a methodical process. They do not rush, preferring to stick to the tried and true methods rather than seeking new adventures. This card can indicate a time when routine and stability are essential.

Practicality & Reliability: This card represents practicality and reliability. The Knight of Pentacles is dependable, trustworthy, and pragmatic, suggesting your situation may benefit from this approach.

Prosperity & Security: On a deeper level, the Knight of Pentacles can signify material wealth and security. It's about working steadily towards your goals to build a secure future.

Stubborn/Inflexible: The Knight of Pentacles is unwavering. Consider if you are staying on course because it makes sense or if you are staying on course because you are unwilling to try something new or a different approach.

QUEEN OF PENTACLES

Overwhelmed by a lack of sustenance and shelter, the raven eventually surrendered to slumber. In its dreamscape, it encountered a nurturing, maternal raven surrounded by a copious variety of food. The air was gently perfumed, enveloping them in a cocoon of tranquility. Lemon trees, their vibrant fruits punctuating the greenery, scattered across the land, exuding an aura of security and prosperity. Dancing among the blossoms, a white rabbit—a symbol of fertility—added to the idyllic scene. In this dream, the raven could shrug off its survival instincts and allow its mind to wander to creative concepts with the potential to manifest abundance. Upon awakening, the raven felt rejuvenated and cherished, ready to implement the innovative ideas birthed from its dream.

Practicality & Sensibility: The Queen of Pentacles is practical and sensible. She is grounded in reality and has a no-nonsense approach to life. This card can signify a situation that would benefit from applying common sense and practical solutions to solve problems.

Nurturing & Generosity: This Queen is a nurturing spirit that exudes generosity. The Queen of Pentacles may enter your situation as a mother figure who provides physical and emotional support. She is caring, warm, and always ready to help those in need.

Abundance & Material Comfort: The Queen of Pentacles is often associated with material wealth and comfort. She is resourceful and knows how to create a comfortable and welcoming environment. This card can signify you are experiencing abundance or focusing on creating a comfortable and secure home.

Connection to the Earth & Nature: This card also signifies a deep connection to the Earth and nature. The Queen of Pentacles appreciates the beauty of the natural world and may also be involved in gardening or other outdoor activities. This card may ask that you feel more connected to nature and the Earth.

Reliability & Trustworthiness: On a deeper level, the Queen of Pentacles embodies the energies of reliability and trustworthiness. She is a loyal friend, a dependable partner, and someone who keeps her promises.

KING OF PENTACLES

In its dream, the raven found its wings bathed in molten gold. As it ascended into the heavens, it unfurled its luminous wings, and tiny droplets transformed into gleaming golden fish. These glittering creatures descended into the lake, reviving the dwindling stock depleted by the forest's residents. In this dream, the raven experienced the delicate balance between giving and receiving, understanding the unimpeded circulation of resources and recognizing that generosity cultivates greater prosperity.

Regardless of how many fish it rained into the water, the raven's golden radiance never diminished; on the contrary, it appeared more brilliant than ever.

Abundance & Prosperity: The King of Pentacles symbolizes financial success and material wealth. He brings the energy of an entrepreneur who has achieved significant wealth and prosperity. This card may appear when you are on the cusp of experiencing financial success or focusing on financial stability.

Stability & Security: The King of Pentacles is dependable, providing a safe and secure environment for his family and loved ones. This card can indicate your need to provide security for others.

Responsibility & Practicality: The King of Pentacles is responsible and practical. He takes his responsibilities seriously and approaches tasks pragmatically and methodically. Your situation may require maintaining your commitments and being accountable for a positive outcome.

Patience & Perseverance: The King of Pentacles asks that you embody patience and perseverance. He knows that success often requires hard work and patience and asks that you stay determined until you achieve your goals.

Enjoyment of the Senses: The King of Pentacles appreciates the finer things in life. He enjoys sensual pleasures and appreciates beauty, quality, and luxury. This card may appear as a sign to enjoy the fruits of your labor and appreciate the material world.

Printed in Dunstable, United Kingdom